2 CORINTHIANS, 1 & 2 TIMOTHY, TITUS:

Ministering in the Spirit and Strength of Jesus

JACK W. HAYFORD

Executive Editor

THOMAS NELSON
Since 1798

NASHVILLE   DALLAS   MEXICO CITY   RIO DE JANEIRO   BEIJING

Published in Nashville, Tennessee. Thomas Nelson is a registered trademark of Thomas Nelson, Inc.

Thomas Nelson, Inc., titles may be purchased in bulk for educational, business, fundraising, or sales promotional use. For information, please email SpecialMarkets@ThomasNelson.com.

Unless otherwise indicated, all Scripture quotations are from the New King James Version, copyright © 1982 by Thomas Nelson, Inc.

Hayford, Jack W.

Ministering in the Spirit

ISBN 13: 978-1-4185-4120-0

Printed in the United States of America
09 10 11 12 13 14 — 6 5 4 3 2 1

TABLE OF CONTENTS

PREFACE
What Would Jesus Do?.. *v*

KEYS OF THE KINGDOM .... *vii*

SESSION ONE
The Human Condition 1

SESSION TWO
The Victor's Way 9

SESSION THREE
Common Instruments of Uncommon Power 19

SESSION FOUR
The Ministry of Reconciliation...................................... 29

SESSION FIVE
Lights in the Darkness 39

SESSION SIX
Overcoming Challenges 53

SESSION SEVEN
The Paradox of Ministry 63

SESSION EIGHT
Spirit-Filled Ministry... 71

SESSION NINE
Prepared to Lead 79

SESSION TEN
   The Good Fight of Faith 89

SESSION ELEVEN
   Committed Ministry 97

SESSION TWELVE
   Renewal 107

CONCLUSION 116

What Would Jesus Do?

IT CAN BE overwhelming to realize all the needs that surround us every day. How can one person make a difference when so much suffering and pain exists? What does it mean to be a channel of God's blessing to others? Can God truly use you to change your world?

The answers to these questions can begin with a very familiar query; ask yourself "What would Jesus do?" This question has been so overused it has nearly lost its meaning. But it continues to be more than relevant to the believer who desires to serve Christ's body on earth and reach beyond to those who remain in darkness. The one who longs to be used of God, to be a channel of His love and healing, must shine forth the image of the Master—Jesus Christ.

Each of us has been given a commission by our Lord: to love as He loves, to serve as He serves, to give our lives for the kingdom of God. To do that, we must be equipped by Him and enabled by Him. We are all called to love and serve; and when God calls, He always enables.

A heart that desires to serve the kingdom is a joy to the Lord for it is a heart attuned to God's. As you work through these pages, stay alert for the still, constant rhythm of God's heart. It is within that glorious pulse that true ministry begins.

Keys of the Kingdom

KEYS CAN BE SYMBOLS of possession, of the right and ability to acquire, clarify, open, or ignite. Keys can be concepts that unleash mind-boggling possibilities. Keys clear the way to a possibility otherwise obstructed!

Jesus spoke of keys: "And I will give you the keys of the kingdom of heaven, and whatever you bind on earth will be bound in heaven, and whatever you loose on earth will be loosed in heaven" (Matthew 16:19).

While Jesus did not define the "keys" He has given, it is clear that He did confer upon His church specific tools that grant us access to a realm of spiritual "partnership" with Him. The "keys" are concepts or biblical themes, traceable throughout Scripture, that are verifiably dynamic when applied with solid faith under the lordship of Jesus Christ. The "partnership" is the essential feature of this enabling grace, allowing believers to receive Christ's promise of "kingdom keys," and to be assured of the Holy Spirit's readiness to actuate their power in the life of the believer.

Faithful students of the Word of God and some of today's most respected Christian leaders have noted some of the primary themes that undergird this spiritual partnership. A concise presentation of many of these primary themes can be found in the Kingdom Dynamics feature of the *New Spirit-Filled Life Bible.* The Spirit-Filled Life Study Guide series, an outgrowth of this Kingdom Dynamics feature, provides a treasury of more in-depth insights on these central truths. This study series offers challenges and insights designed to enable you to more readily understand and appropriate certain dynamic KINGDOM KEYS.

Each study guide has twelve to fourteen lessons, and a number of helpful features have been developed to assist you in your study, each marked by a symbol and heading for easy identification.

Kingdom Key

KINGDOM KEY identifies the foundational Scripture passage for each study session and highlights a basic concept or principle presented in the text along with cross-referenced passages.

Kingdom Life

The KINGDOM LIFE feature is designed to give practical understanding and insight. This feature will assist you in comprehending the truths contained in Scripture and applying them to your day-to-day needs, hurts, relationships, concerns, or circumstances.

Word Wealth

The WORD WEALTH feature provides important definitions of key terms.

Behind the Scenes

BEHIND THE SCENES supplies information about cultural beliefs and practices, doctrinal disputes, and various types of background information that will illuminate Bible passages and teachings.

Kingdom Extra

The optional KINGDOM EXTRA feature will guide you to Bible dictionaries, Bible encyclopedias, and other resources that will enable you to gain further insight into a given topic.

Probing the Depths

Finally, PROBING THE DEPTHS will present any controversial issues raised by particular lessons and cite Bible passages and other sources that will assist you in arriving at your own conclusions.

Each volume of the Spirit-Filled Life Study Guide series is a comprehensive resource presenting study and life-application questions and exercises with spaces provided for recording your answers. These study guides are designed to provide all you need to gain a good, basic understanding of the covered theme and apply biblical counsel to your life. You will need only a heart and mind open to the Holy Spirit, a prayerful attitude, a pencil and a Bible to complete the studies and apply the truths they contain. However, you may want to have a notebook handy if you plan to expand your study to include the optional KINGDOM EXTRA feature.

The Bible study method used in this series employs four basic steps:

1. *Observation.* What does the text say?
2. *Interpretation.* What is the original meaning of the text?
3. *Correlation.* What light can be shed on this text by other Scripture passages?
4. *Application.* How should my life change in response to the Holy Spirit's teaching of this text?

The New King James Version is the translation used wherever Scripture portions are cited in the Spirit-Filled Life Study Guide series. Using this translation with this series will make your study easier, but it is certainly not imperative and you will profit through use of any translation you choose.

Through Bible study, you will grow in your essential understanding of the Lord, His kingdom and your place in it; but you need more. Jesus was sent to teach us "all things" (John 14:25–26). Rely on the Holy Spirit to guide your study and your application of the Bible's truths. Bathe your study time in prayer as you use this series to learn of Him and His plan for your life. Ask the Spirit of God to illuminate the text, enlighten your mind, humble your will, and comfort your heart. And as you explore the Word of God and find the keys to unlock its riches, may the Holy Spirit fill every fiber of your being with the joy and power God longs to give all His children. Read diligently on. Stay open and submissive to Him. Learn to live your life as the Creator intended. You will not be disappointed. He promises you!

ADDITIONAL OBSERVATIONS

SESSION ONE

The Human Condition

2 Corinthians 1:1—2:11

 Kingdom Key—*Weakness = Strength*

2 Corinthians 12:9 My grace is sufficient for you, for My strength is made perfect in weakness.

Grace is God's unmerited favor—a manifestation of His power, exceeding what we could achieve or hope for by our own labors. It is a God-given resource that makes our salvation and "holy living" possible when life, circumstance, or character is under fire by the adversary. God's grace becomes His enablement or empowerment to achieve His plan, endure hardship, overcome adversity, or access Him. Paul's struggle, his "thorn in the flesh" (2 Corinthians 12:7), has never been defined with certainty, so that any one of us may find God's words to him equally applicable to us. His grace is powerful and all-enabling to the believer. His grace facilitates our abilities to conquer every weakness as we yield to an absolute trust and reliance upon God, trusting His heart even when we cannot trace His hand. God gives us grace—the supernatural ability, or miraculous faculty, to sustain, endure, or maintain our call—for all He is enabling us to become in Christ.

Read 1 Corinthians 1:26–31; 2 Thessalonians 1:11–12; James 4:6–10.

Questions:

How do you understand strength and God's grace to be interconnected?

_____

_____

_____

In what way have you experienced God's strengthening in your life?

✎ _____

_____

The Church at Corinth

The apostle Paul faced a seemingly impossible mission. God had called him to plant a church in first-century Corinth, a leading commercial center of southern Greece. It was a wide-open boomtown similar to San Francisco in the gold rush days. The church was filled with new converts saved out of the pagan world of Corinth, famous for its immorality and loose living. Like any cosmopolitan city, Corinth was a mixture of different races and cultures, and the Corinthian church had its difficulties with factions and instabilities. False teachers and power-hungry church members compounded the problems faced by this fledgling church.

The call of God on Paul's life required that he not only plant churches, but that he oversee and continue to minister to these early Christian assemblies. His experiences, as they are expressed through this letter, offer anyone called into ministry at any level the rare opportunity of observing how a ministry continues in the Spirit and strength of Jesus.

Kingdom Life—*Recognize True Ministry*

Second Corinthians shows Paul to be a down-to-earth apostle who faced challenges in ministry similar to those we face today. Paul was not an unapproachable or holier-than-thou saint. Like us, he had weaknesses and personal struggles. Neither was Paul revered by all as we might expect. On the contrary, Paul was in some respects so utterly human, so merely normal, that some super-spiritual believers disdained and dishonored him. These people were mesmerized by style over substance, and in their disappointment at not finding the ministry style they wanted in Paul, they failed to recognize that Paul was representing Jesus Christ to and among them most faithfully.

Paul's response to these challenges demonstrates how God delights in expressing His strength through human weakness. This divine choice is expressed clearly in the cross of Jesus and also, in a way that is practical for believers and spiritual leaders today, in the experience and example of Paul.

Throughout 2 Corinthians, Paul contrasts ministry that is true to the spirit of Jesus and that is sustained by His strength against ministry that expresses a worldly, self-serving spirit and that is sustained by worldly ideas of strength and power.

Read Philippians 2:1–4.

Questions:

In ministering to others, do you find yourself speaking often as though you have "arrived"?

_____

_____

What effect do you think this has on others?

_____

_____

What does it say about you?

_____

_____

What do you suppose causes this way of thinking and speaking?

_____

_____

Word Wealth—*Comfort*

Comfort: Greek *paraklesis* (par-ak'-lay-sis); Strong's *#3874*: means a calling alongside to help, to comfort, to console or encourage. The *paraklete* is a strengthening presence, one who upholds those appealing for assistance. *Paraklēsis* (comfort) can come to us both by the Holy Spirit and by the Scriptures.

Kingdom Life—*Comforted to Be a Comfort*

A recent poll among evangelical Christian pastors revealed that a significant percentage felt emotionally isolated and discouraged, doubted their call to ministry, and considered leaving it. Whether you are in full-time ministry or actively ministering as a lay member of the body of Christ, discouragement and isolation can seriously diminish effective ministry. Paul's response to the difficulties at Corinth points spiritual leaders and all believers to the resource that will sustain them in any challenge.

Paul was commissioned by God to be an apostle, an assignment he was able to fulfill only by knowing the reality of the *paraklete* and understanding the God of all comfort. By properly defining the concept of "comfort," we can understand how we live the Christian life, which is impossible in merely human strength and wisdom.

Read Psalm 71:20–21; John 15:26; 2 Corinthians 1:3–7; Acts 9:31; Romans 15:4–6.

Questions:

What ways does God use to comfort us?

_____

_____

_____

How can this increase our effectiveness in ministry?

_____

_____

When have you experienced the Holy Spirit as Comforter in your life?

_____

_____

Kingdom Extra

Paul teaches us that the God "who comforts us in all our tribulation" (2 Corinthians 1:4) strengthens us supernaturally. The secret of Paul's strength was also known and experienced by Isaiah the prophet. Both Paul and Isaiah wrote about ordinary believers or Christian leaders seeking the presence of the Lord in the midst of the demands and pressures of life. His presence consoles, comforts, and strengthens. From this place of rest and delight with the Lord, the fountainhead of true ministry rises. Comforted by the Lord, believers can comfort others.

Read Isaiah 40:31.

Questions:

Although God can and does comfort people directly through His Holy Spirit, why do you think it is important that we encourage one another?

✎ _____

_____

Why is it vitally important that we find practical ways to honor, uphold, and even defend (if need be) those who minister to others in our midst?

✎ _____

Ministry Is Others-Centered

Second Corinthians is the most autobiographical of all Paul's letters. It contains numerous references to the hardships he endured in the course of his ministry. It is in this letter that Paul strenuously defends his ministry and gives definition to true spirituality.

In defending his ministry, Paul opens his heart, showing his deep emotion. He reveals his strong love for the Corinthians, his ardent zeal for the glory of God, his uncompromising loyalty to the truth of the gospel, and his stern indignation in confronting those who were disrupting the fellowship of the church. His life was bound up in his converts, and he was passionately involved in their growth in the kingdom. No price was too great if the result was glorifying God and advancing His kingdom.

Read 2 Corinthians 1:1—2:11.

Questions:

What qualities did you discover in Paul that were imperative to his powerful ministry?

✎ _____

_____

Which of these qualities do you find in yourself?

✎ _____

Which qualities do you lack and how does that negatively affect your own ministry?

_____

_____

"Yes" Means "Yes"

At the core of integrity, of straightforwardness, is character—being people of our word, people whose "yes" means simply "yes" and not "yes and no" at the same time. Fickle people are not stable; they do not have integrity and can't be counted on to lead or follow reliably. If you do not follow through on your word, you cannot be trusted and what you promise will be suspect. To speak one thing and do another is no different than a lie.

Read Matthew 21:28–31.

Questions:

Are you a person of integrity?

_____

_____

How is this shown in your life?

_____

_____

_____

How might you improve in this area?

_____

_____

_____

Probing the Depths

Church discipline may be the most difficult of all tasks for a minister and a church. It is challenging enough when a member's error is persistent, flagrant sin; but the case Paul has to deal with is even thornier. Paul's motives for ministry were

SESSION TWO

The Victor's Way

2 Corinthians 2:12—3:18

Kingdom Key—*Triumph in Christ*

Romans 8:37 Yet in all these things we are more than conquerors through Him who loved us.

Perhaps you have heard of the old expression, "I have been down so long, everything looks up to me"; or "If life's a bowl of cherries, why do I feel like I'm in the pits?" Both of these expressions reflect a deep weariness, even despair, that many feel today. If not responded to properly, disappointments, tragedies, hurts, rejections, lost opportunities, and setbacks can produce a cynical and negative state of mind that is not biblical. The apostle Paul was clearly no stranger to difficulty and disappointment. Yet, in the midst of adversity, Paul thanks the God "who always leads us in triumph in Christ" (2 Corinthians 2:14).

Such triumph transcends mere positive thinking or simply keeping a good attitude. Paul understood the adversity in his life in the greater context of God's master plan for him. He realized that as he continually sought the Lord, God was ordering events behind the scenes for his good. Paul did not become fatalistic, nor did he roll over and play dead in the face of adverse circumstances. Paul "fought the good fight" (2 Timothy 4:7) and employed powerful spiritual weapons. But most of all, Paul was empowered by the Holy Spirit. He was open to and walked in the presence of God, and the resurrection power of Christ carried him through circumstances under which we stumble and fall in our own strength.

Read Psalm 42:11; Romans 8:28, 38–39.

Questions:

Have you ever felt despair or defeat in your walk with the Lord?

What steps can you take to combat those deceitful and harmful reactions?

Find Scripture portions that give further direction in defeating defeat.

Behind the Scenes

In 2 Corinthians 2:14–16, Paul may have been alluding to the Roman victory parade that was common in his day. In this parade both the conquering and the defeated leaders marched down the street, along with the victorious army and their captives. Fragrant spices were burned along the route as part of the festivities. However, the same aroma meant different things to victor and vanquished. To the defeated the fragrance was an aroma leading to death, because execution or slavery (to some, a fate worse than death) surely followed. For the triumphant, however, the aroma was altogether lovely, marking their victory, triumph, and life. Paul's point is that in Christ he and all believers are part of God's victory parade, even in the midst of anxieties and all manner of difficulty.

Effectiveness in Ministry

Our effectiveness in ministering to others is directly related to our integrity and sincerity. We must allow the Holy Spirit to purify our motives when we minister to others. Tragically, today as in Paul's day, some people do not preach the gospel from pure motives, but in order to gain wealth and power.

All ministers of the gospel who aim to be faithful at some point feel the force of the urgency of the gospel, of the need for lost humanity to hear and obey the gospel, and of the various natural, human, and demonic forces that hinder the effective spread of the gospel. They recognize how the ministry of the gospel requires, finally, supernatural empowerment.

Read Colossians 1:24–29; Hebrews 6:10–12; 1 Peter 4:8–11.

Questions:

What does it mean to be a minister of the gospel?

_____

Why are integrity and sincerity imperative to effective ministry?

_____

In what ways are you called to minister to the body of Christ?

_____

_____

What steps might you take to increase the effectiveness of this ministry?

_____

_____

_____

Probing the Depths

In Paul's time, *peddling* referred to the work of small-time, unethical traders whom we would call hucksters today. Some of their dishonesty would include, for example, diluting good wine with water or using false weights in order to make an excessive profit on merchandise. Peddlers (from *kapēleuō*, Strong's #2585) were contrasted with legitimate merchants (from *emporos*, Strong's #1713).

Although the majority of Christian ministers and ministries are working for Jesus Christ sincerely, some fall into the trap of being concerned more with raising money than with ministering the life of Jesus to others. Even well-meaning religious enterprises can be caught up in the pursuit of money, power, prestige, and influence, if they are not constantly holding themselves accountable and submitting themselves to the Lord Jesus Christ and to others in His body.

The Evangelical Council for Financial Accountability was founded in 1979 and provides accreditation "to leading Christian nonprofit organizations that faithfully demonstrate compliance with seven Standards of Responsible Stewardship, including financial accountability, fund-raising and board governance." According to the council's Web site, collectively, the revenue of these leading Christian nonprofit organizations totals in excess of $18 billion per year.

Before supporting an organization with which you are unfamiliar, you may wish to visit the ECFA Web site (www.efca.org) to discover whether the organization is a member in good standing.

Read Romans 12:1–18; 1 Corinthians 13:1–3; Philippians 2:1–4.

Questions:

What motivates you to minister the gospel?

_____

_____

_____

Do you use ministry in any way for personal gain (position or favor)?

_____

_____

_____

What steps can you take to purify your heart and mind as a minister of the gospel?

_____

_____

Kingdom Life—*Minister in Truth and Life*

Believing in the truthfulness of God's Word does not guarantee that we will minister that truth in the Spirit of God. We learn in Ephesians 4:15 that growth and maturity in the body of Christ is directly related to "speaking the truth in love." Paul warns us in 2 Corinthians 3:6 that there is danger in ministering God's truth literally without imparting life.

The Spirit of truth (1 John 4:6) and the Spirit of life (Romans 8:2) are the same—the Holy Spirit! Blending truth and life will always result in three things:

1. *A faithfulness to keep straight.* "Rightly dividing the word of truth" (2 Timothy 2:15) means putting forward the truth faithfully and forthrightly. (This verse was never intended to refer to "dividing" the Word by segmenting it, but rather to a straight-forward dealing with all the truth and all its implications.)

2. *A constant presence of love, even in the most demanding declarations of correction.* Urgency may attend our message and passion infuse our delivery, but no matter how literally accurate our interpretation and delivery of biblical truth, anger, impatience, and irritation are not of the Spirit of God.

3. *Jesus promised signs to follow the preaching of God's Word.* The early church experienced these signs, and Paul described the evidence of signs as the norm in his ministry (1 Corinthians 2:1–5; 1 Thessalonians 1:5). Hebrews 2:1–4 confirms that signs and wonders verify Christ's living presence and serve to warn believers against drifting away from the new life to which we have been called. Our hearts should be enlarged by the Holy Spirit with a passionate love for others.

Read John 13:34–35; 14:12–14; 15:9–27; 1 Peter 1:22–23.

Questions:

What are the results of ministry offered without love?

Is true love a matter of feelings and emotions?

_____

_____

_____

How do decision and choice come into play in real love?

_____

_____

Kingdom Extra

The work of God among the Corinthians was one of the evidences of the legitimacy and divine authority of Paul's ministry. Yet Paul had to defend his authority at Corinth because his leadership was being challenged by others who were trying to control the church. The difference between Paul and his rivals was that Paul's authority came from God. His credentials validating his claim to be a legitimate minister of Christ were the Corinthians themselves. Their lives gave evidence that they were a living letter of recommendation regarding his ministry. Unlike Paul's opponents, who were trying to promote themselves, Paul did not need some kind of formal letter of introduction and recommendation. The proof of his ministry was the changed lives of the Corinthians.

Denominational accreditation, ministerial credentials, and theological training can all have a place in ministry. But what is the final proof of our legitimacy in ministry (2 Corinthians 3:1–6)?

A Superior Covenant

After Paul established the church in Corinth, other missionaries visited them. Apparently, these late-comer missionaries honored the old covenant as "holy and just and good" (Romans 7:12) and as the unerring revealer of sin. But unlike Paul, these ministers had more confidence in the ability of the old covenant to promote life in Christ. In answer to their attempts to discredit his ministry, Paul highlights the superiority of God's new covenant through Jesus and the ministry that serves this new covenant.

Paul wanted the Corinthian church to realize that despite any dislike of his personal style, his ministry was authentic and deserving of the honor due the covenant he ministered. Correspondingly, the mixed new-plus-old-covenant ministry of his opponents was inferior, despite how much any of the Corinthians might have preferred the personal style of such ministers. The true worth of a ministry is determined by the worth of the covenant one ministers, not by personal preferences that make up ministerial style. It is important to note that Paul does not belittle the old covenant but that he exalts the new covenant.

Probing the Depths

Christians differ in their convictions about how the old covenant continues to be important for life under the new covenant, and these differences appear within the New Testament itself. For example, the differences in matters of conscience that Paul addresses in Romans 14 and 15 arise from how believers feel the force of old covenant commandments differently upon their lives in Christ.

Read Matthew 5:17–20; 22:37–40; Romans 3:19–31; 13:8–10; Galatians 5:1–6, 13–18.

Questions:

What do you see as the continuing role of the old covenant (and its law) in the Christian life?

✎_____

_____

_____

How should it (or should it not) affect your daily life?

✎_____

_____

Kingdom Extra

While Paul contrasts the old and new covenants in the compact verses of 2 Corinthians 3:6–18, nearly all of the book of Hebrews contrasts the two to show how much better the new covenant is and to urge believers not to waver in their confidence in this new and living way. For a quick overview, look up the following references and complete the table displaying the points at which the new covenant is superior to the old.

Passage	What from the New Covenant	Is Superior to	What from the Old Covenant?
Heb. 1:5–14	Jesus		
Heb. 3:1–6			
Heb. 4:1–11			a rest never entered into
Heb. 7:14—8:6			
Heb. 9:7–12; 10:1–4, 22			
Heb. 9:7–8, 15–17			

Kingdom Extra

When Moses came down from the mountain after personally encountering God, he wore a literal veil over his face to prevent the children of Israel from seeing the full manifestation of God's glory. He removed this veil when he was in the presence of the Lord but put it back on when he went back to talk to the children of Israel. Paul gave two reasons for Moses' use of the veil:

1. To mute the radiance of the glory on his face so the people could look at him.
2. To prevent their disappointment when the glory began to fade away.

Then Paul transformed the literal veil into a spiritual symbol, and he moved it from the face of Moses to the hearts of those who know God only through Moses, even when One greater than Moses had come, namely Jesus Christ. To this day, when such physical children of Israel, modern Jews, read their Hebrew Bible and reject Christ, this veil mutes the full glory of God's Word. Because Jesus is the living Word of God, only by accepting Him for who God says He is can the veil be removed. But for those who do turn to the Lord, God's Spirit liberates them from a muted, vanishing glory and transmits to them the life-giving and life-transforming permanent glory of God that shines from the face of Jesus.

Read Exodus 34:29–35.

Question:

In what three ways does our worship of God and the accompanying release of His glory on our lives affect our ability to share our faith with others?

✎ _____

_____

_____

Record Your Thoughts

Consider this comment on 2 Corinthians 3:18 from the *Spirit-Filled Life Bible*: " 'Beholding as in a mirror' connotes 'reflecting' as well as 'looking into.' As we behold 'the glory of the Lord,' we are continually 'transformed into the same image' by 'the Spirit of the Lord.' We, then, with ever-increasing glory, reflect what we behold." Ponder the last sentence of that note. What significance for corporate and personal worship can you see in it?

Questions:

How can you behold the Lord more in your life?

✎ _____

_____

_____

_____

What can you behold less in order that you might behold Him more?

✎ _____

_____

_____

_____

Spend some time worshipping the Lord either privately or at church and do the following:

- Praise and worship the Lord and allow His presence to fill your heart and soul.
- Delight in His presence and thank Him specifically for things that He has done in your life.
- Be conscious of His presence and allow Him to speak to you.
- Give Him any burdens you may be carrying and place them in His hands.
- Let His glory fill you and allow His glory to minister to and through you.
- As you are experiencing His glory, *expect* that He will release you from any bondage, anxiety, oppression, or fear that may be in your life.
- Know that 2 Corinthians 3:17 is a present reality: "Where the Spirit of the Lord is, there is liberty."

When you spend time beholding the Lord, you will discover that you will be released in many different dimensions in your life.

SESSION THREE

Common Instruments of Uncommon Power

2 Corinthians 4

 Kingdom Key—*Be God's Tool*

Isaiah 6:8 I heard the voice of the Lord, saying: "Whom shall I send, and who will go for Us?"

Then I said, "Here am I! Send me."

"Who will go for Us?" God uses a few words to communicate a very deep and profound truth. When we embark upon a life of ministry (whether by vocation or layman's call), we go about our Father's business. We serve Him by touching the lives of others. We serve others because we love Him. If ministry exists for any reason but this, it is not ministry, but self-promotion; it is not love, but pride; not service, but using others to promote our own agenda.

Read Matthew 7:21–23; 25:31–46.

Questions:

Have you ever been hurt by someone "ministering" their own agenda?

_____

_____

How can you guard against this in your own life?

_____

_____

_____

Kingdom Life—*Mercy Is Required*

The word translated as *mercy* in 2 Corinthians 4:1 is the Greek *eleos* ([el'-eh-oss] Strong's *#1656*). It means compassion, tender mercy, kindness, beneficence, and an outward manifestation of pity.

Mercy is the aspect of God's love that causes Him to help the needy or those in miserable, rejected, or unfortunate situations, just as grace is the aspect of His love that moves Him to forgive the guilty. Those who are miserable may be so either because of breaking God's law or because of circumstances beyond their control.

God shows mercy upon those who have broken His law (Daniel 9:9; 1 Timothy 1:13, 16). God's mercy on the needy or miserable extends beyond punishment that is withheld (Ephesians 2:4–6). Withheld punishment keeps us from deserved judgment, but it does not necessarily grant blessing. God's mercy is greater than this.

God also shows mercy by actively helping those who are needy or in miserable straits due to circumstances beyond their control. We see this aspect of mercy especially in the life of our Lord Jesus when He healed those who suffered physically. These acts of healing grew out of His commitment to reveal the will of God through acts of mercy.

Because God is merciful, He expects His children to be merciful. Read Matthew 5:7; 12:7; 23:23; Luke 10:37.

Questions:

Would others describe you as merciful?

✐ _____

_____

How does mercy find expression in your ministry to others?

✐ _____

_____

How can lack of mercy adversely affect your ministry?

✐ _____

_____

Word Wealth—*Craftiness*

Craftiness: Greek *panourgia* (pan-oorg-ee'-ah); Strong's #*3834*: Means versatile cleverness, astute knavery, sophisticated cunning, unscrupulous conduct, evil treachery, deceptive scheming, arrogant shrewdness, and sly arrogance. Used only five times in the New Testament, it refers to Satan's deceiving Eve (2 Corinthians 11:3); the Pharisees' trying to trick Jesus (Luke 20:23); the deception of false teachers (Ephesians 4:14); the self-entrapment of the worldly wise (1 Corinthians 3:19); and the improper method of presenting the gospel (2 Corinthians 4:2).

The Wisdom of the World

"Craftiness" (2 Corinthians 4:2) describes the kind of thinking and behavior that God does not want His people to adopt. This behavior employs the "wisdom of this world" (1 Corinthians 3:19), and is far removed from the wisdom that comes from God. All of us have known schemers and manipulators who attempt to engineer things for their own advantage, getting people to do things through trickery, manipulation, or deceit. Our society is permeated with that kind of thinking as demonstrated by certain politicians, salespeople, and advertisers, who deceive and manipulate others (knowingly or not) to accomplish their own goals. In many ways, our culture has lost its ability to discern truth from error. As a result, we often exalt image over substance. But this is not how God wants His people to behave. Christians are to be people of openness, accountability, and integrity in a dark world.

Probing the Depths

In the past fifty years, the culture of our nation has moved further and further away from traditional Christian values. The freedom movement of the 1960s has grown into a culture wherein right and wrong are dependent upon circumstance and absolutes are deemed restrictive and unenlightened. Christianity is considered by many, especially in media, to be restrictive, elitist, and intolerant. Biblical truth has often been watered down or completely rejected by a liberal society in the name of tolerance and politically correct attitudes and responses.

This significant shift in our society's perception of Christianity was propelled yet further by the televangelist scandals and the consequent fall of a number of prominent TV evangelists. What happened impacted the Christian culture at large, in that Satan secured a stronghold in the consciousness of our nation and world. The deceptive, manipulative, materialistic, and immoral actions of a few media personalities resulted in the Christian world being perceived as hypocritical, uninformed, and easily deceived.

The world today is exposed to almost nothing in the popular media besides stereotypes of Christian ministers portrayed as harshly judgmental, immoral, deceitful, or bland and bumbling. The first way to deal with this false perception, or stronghold, in popular culture is for ordinary Christians and ministers to conduct themselves with integrity, intelligence, accountability, and transparency. The second, and most important, way to deal with this stronghold is to fast and pray for our nation and ask God to tear down this stronghold erected by the Enemy. (See 2 Corinthians 10:4–5.)

Read Psalms 7:8–9; 26:1–6; Proverbs 10:9–12; 11:2–3; Titus 2:6–7.

Questions:

What are some examples of how a Christian might walk in "craftiness" (2 Corinthians 4:2), especially in ministry?

_____

How do you define *integrity*?

_____

_____

What are the consequences of walking without integrity?

_____

_____

In what ways can you guard against a lack of integrity in your walk with the Lord and your ministry for Him?

Word Wealth—*Conscience*

Conscience: Greek *suneidesis* (soon-i'-day-sis); Strong's #*4893*: Refers to a person's inner awareness of conforming to the will of God or departing from it, resulting in either a sense of approval or condemnation. It literally means "a knowing," a coknowledge with one's self, the witness borne to one's conduct by conscience, that faculty by which we apprehend the will of God.

In the New Testament "conscience" is found most frequently in Paul's epistles. However, the conscience is by no means the final standard of moral goodness. The conscience is trustworthy only when formed by the Word and will of God. The law given to Israel was inscribed on the hearts of believers, so the sensitized conscience is able to discern God's judgment against sin.

The conscience of the believer has been cleansed by the work of Jesus Christ; it no longer accuses and condemns. Believers are to maintain pure consciences and not encourage others to act against their consciences. To act contrary to the urging of one's conscience is wrong, for actions that go against the conscience cannot arise out of faith.

Read Romans 2:14–15; 1 Corinthians 8; 10:23–33; Hebrews 8:10; 9:14; 10:16–22.

Questions:

What is the connection between faith and conscience?

How does conscience come into play in ministry?

Can you think of a time when ignoring the prompting of your conscience resulted in negative consequences?

✎ _____

_____

_____

What part does the Word of God play in a healthy conscience toward God?

✎ _____

_____

_____

Kingdom Life—*From Glory to Glory*

If a Christian does not spend time contemplating the glory and majesty of the Lord, there will not be life-changing power in his life. The reason we have so many weak Christians is that they spend their time filling their minds and hearts with the things of this world.

We need a sanctuary. We need something to think upon that will clean up our minds. The Word of God is a mirror, and in it we behold the glory of the Lord. The only way you can behold the living Christ is in the Word of God. As you behold Him, there is a liberty, a freedom, and a growth that He gives you. Your life is changed and empowered as you develop a more intimate relationship with Jesus. You cannot come by it in any other way.

Read Philippians 4:8.

Questions:

This verse has been called the briefest biography of Christ. Why do you believe this is so?

✎ _____

_____

_____

How much time do you spend contemplating Christ and reading the Word of God?

✎ _____

What impact does this have on your ability to live out your faith?

✎ _____

What impact does this have on your ability to minister to others?

✎ _____

_____

How can you make sure you are magnifying Christ in your life and ministry?

✎ _____

_____

_____

Treasure in Earthen Vessels

"But we have this treasure in earthen vessels, that the excellence of the power may be of God and not of us" (2 Corinthians 4:7).

Have you ever felt disqualified for spiritual service? Have you ever wondered if God really could ever use you? The apostle Paul understood those feelings, and that's why he wrote these words. Sometimes when we look at people in public ministry, it's easy to get the wrong impression of what ministry is all about. They may seem to be above human frailty and beyond the failings we all experience. However, we don't get to see those people right after they just wake up in the morning or after a hard day's work or when the dishwasher breaks and the kids are screaming.

These people live in the same world you and I do. They have

problems, faults, and shortcomings just like all of us. They do not walk around on some spiritual cloud going from victory to victory. All of us are just ordinary people with human weaknesses and shortcomings. But the good news is that God can still use each one of us because effectiveness does not depend on us, but on the quality of the covenant we represent, so "that the excellence of the power may be of God and not of us" (2 Corinthians 4:7).

God delights in taking ordinary people and doing something absolutely tremendous with their lives. This truth can free us from the bondage of trying to perform perfectly. Our job is not to be perfect (as a performer of ministry), but to trust in and cooperate with the Holy Spirit at work in and through us. As we walk with Him, He can take our ordinariness and manifest His extraordinary power.

Read Romans 8:1–17.

Questions:

According to this Scripture, what enables effective ministry?

_____

_____

How do we "put to death" the "deeds of the body" (Romans 8:13)?

_____

_____

_____

Is the Spirit of God made manifest in your life and ministry? In what ways?

_____

_____

_____

What steps can you take to increase the flow of God's power in and through your life?

_____

_____

Kingdom Extra

"Earthen vessels" (2 Corinthians 4:7) refers to the widespread use of clay for all kinds of household containers—jugs, pots, pans, and cups. The clay was common and unimpressive, fragile and easily broken. Yet people would regularly store valuables in them, just as God has placed His treasure in ministers of the new covenant who, like Paul, seem quite common and unimpressive to folks viewing things through the lenses of worldly values.

Read 2 Corinthians 4:7–10; Galatians 6:17.

Questions:

How can you carry "about in the body the dying of the Lord Jesus" (2 Corinthians 4:10)?

_____

_____

_____

How is the life of Jesus made manifest in your life and ministry?

_____

_____

Kingdom Life—*Focus on the Eternal*

Paul proclaimed that, regardless of circumstance, he would not lose heart. Because of his faith in the future resurrection and because of his very real experience of God's renewing power, Paul continued to preach with courage and determination. This is a powerful example to all who will minister in the name and power of our Lord.

Though the circumstances surrounding us may look less than promising, we "do not look" (2 Corinthians 4:18) at them. This does not mean that we ignore reality, but that we do not focus our attention on the outward, perishing world. By faith we must see more than the outward and more than the present. We must clearly see temporary things in the clarifying light of the eternal.

Record Your Thoughts

Reread 2 Corinthians 4:16–18 and try to put in your own words the core truths Paul expresses.

_____

_____

_____

_____

Questions:

How can focusing on the eternal affect the way you look at the adversities you face in ministry?

_____

_____

_____

_____

How would the Spirit of God lead you to respond to criticism of your walk with the Lord or your ministry?

_____

_____

_____

How has this section changed your view of the way you live out the ministry to which the Lord has called you?

_____

_____

_____

SESSION FOUR

The Ministry of Reconciliation

2 Corinthians 5

Kingdom Key—*It's All About Jesus*

Colossians 3:17 Whatever you do in word or deed, do all in the name of the Lord Jesus, giving thanks to God the Father through Him.

The entire Christian experience is wrapped up in the resurrection of Jesus Christ. Men can have all kinds of intellectual arguments and philosophies that attempt to argue against the truth of the gospel of Jesus Christ. But if Jesus Christ rose from the dead, then all of these arguments come to nothing, because that which is universally agreed to be humanly impossible—to die and then come to life again, never to die again—has happened. The truth of the resurrection is so important that the apostle Paul declared, "If Christ is not risen, then our preaching is empty and your faith is also empty" (1 Corinthians 15:14).

The power and authority of the gospel stem from the fact that Jesus Christ really did rise from the dead in real space, time, and history. This occurrence of the resurrection in regular time and space is what separates Jesus Christ from every other spiritual teacher, guru, and prophet throughout history. The Buddha, Muhammad, and all the other spiritual teachers are still dead. Only Jesus Christ rose from the dead as the unique Son of God.

Read Colossians 1:9–23.

Questions:

What does it mean for Christ to have "preeminence" (Colossians 1:18)?

Is this true in your ministry?

_____

_____

Kingdom Life—*Jesus Is Our Foundation*

Reconciliation is the process by which God and man are brought together again. This is made possible through the blood of Jesus, which demonstrates the power and the model for reconciliation. We were once estranged from Him, but we have been brought to God and restored to relationship through the shed blood of Christ; His power is fueled in us through the body of His flesh through His death. As children of God and joint heirs with Jesus Christ, we are enjoined to follow the standard He left for us—to be reconciled to God and with each other as He reconciled us to God. As we model His ministry of reconciliation, the world will be impacted.

Read Romans 5:10; Colossians 1:19–22; Ephesians 2:12–13.

Questions:

What do you understand the term "spirit of reconciliation" to mean?

_____

_____

Is the spirit of reconciliation alive and well in your life and ministry?

_____

_____

How might the increase of this conciliatory force impact your service to the Lord?

_____

_____

Kingdom Extra

Jesus rose from death! This fact is the cornerstone of the Christian faith. The New Testament itself exists only because its several writers were absolutely sure that

Jesus had risen. Most, if not all, of its writers were eyewitnesses of the risen Lord. Christ appeared after the resurrection numerous times.

When Paul condensed the heart of Christian belief to a few affirmations (1 Corinthians 15:1–7), he mentioned that more than five hundred persons saw Christ after His resurrection. Many of those were yet alive when Paul wrote this passage of Scripture. As a result, our belief in the resurrection rests on the testimony of a great number of people who had firsthand knowledge.

But our belief goes even beyond such historical eyewitnesses. In His final words to some of His followers before He ascended to heaven, Jesus told those historical eyewitnesses that they needed something else in order to be the kind of witnesses He wanted them to be: "He commanded them not to depart from Jerusalem, but to wait for the Promise of the Father . . . ," and He said, "You shall receive power when the Holy Spirit has come upon you; and you shall be witnesses to Me in Jerusalem, and in all Judea and Samaria, and to the end of the earth" (Acts 1:4, 8). God wants us to believe that Jesus rose again for two main reasons:

1. Because we accept the sincere testimony of historical eyewitnesses who became effective spiritual witnesses by being filled with the Holy Spirit.
2. By becoming witnesses ourselves of the fact that He is risen from the dead through experiencing the same outpouring of His Spirit, which is the Spirit of our ascended, exalted Lord (Acts 2:32–33). The outpoured Spirit makes unrepeatable, historical truth a contemporary, ongoing event in the lives of believers today.

Read Luke 24:29–33; John 20:19–28; 21:1–19; Acts 9:1–22.

Questions:

What do Jesus' words to Thomas as recorded in John 20 mean to you personally?

✎ _____

_____

_____

How is the truth of Jesus' resurrection a viable aspect of your walk with Him?

_____

_____

What are the implications of Jesus' resurrection for daily life?

_____

_____

Word Wealth—*Judgment Seat*

Judgment Seat: Greek *bema* (bay'-ma); Strong's *#968*: From the root word *baino,* "to go," the word originally described a step or a stride. Then it was used for a raised platform reached by steps, especially from which orations were made. Later, it denoted the tribune or tribunal of a ruler where litigants stood trial. In the New Testament it usually refers to earthly magistrates (Acts 18:12, 16–17), but twice it is used of the divine tribunal before which believers will stand (Romans 14:10; 2 Corinthians 5:10).

Kingdom Life—*We Are Accountable Before God*

The central message of the gospel is that we are saved entirely by faith and not through any kind of human effort. The Bible teaches us that there is absolutely nothing we can do to earn salvation.

However, many people who believe that they are saved by faith are not clear about what Scripture says about their accountability before God and what the Bible calls the "judgment seat of Christ" (2 Corinthians 5:10). Every believer in Jesus Christ will stand before this judgment. We are personally accountable before God for what we do with our lives after we are saved; held responsible for faithfulness as parents, husbands, wives, children, employees, ministers, and citizens. God has invested many things into every one of our lives, and He expects us to be fruitful for His kingdom.

It is important that we do not misunderstand Scripture here. It's not that we are trying to sneak religious works back into the salvation picture. But the Bible does teach that all believers are directly accountable to God for what they have done with their time, talents, and abilities.

Jesus may not return today or tomorrow, but He is going to return. In that day when He returns, Christians will also be judged. Our judgment will not determine whether or not we will be saved. This will not be a criminal court, but a civil court where our property will be in danger. He will judge us in order to see if we are worthy or not to receive rewards. There will be degrees of rewards for the believer just as there will be degrees of punishment for the unbeliever.

Read Matthew 25:14–46; Luke 12:42–48; 19:12–27; John 5:25–27; Acts 10:42; Ephesians 2:4–10; Revelation 22:12.

Questions:

In your own words, briefly explain how you can be saved by grace and yet still be accountable before God for your life choices.

✎ _____

_____

What do you believe would be the verdict if you stood before the judgment seat of Christ today?

✎ _____

_____

Locate other Scriptures that describe the judgment of the redeemed.

✎ _____

_____

What convictions do you experience in reading these words of truth?

✎ _____

_____

What changes do you believe the Lord would have you make in this regard in order to minister His truth to others more effectively?

✎ _____

_____

Behind the Scenes

A major emphasis of Jesus' teaching is how to build and maintain relationships with God and others. He views these relationships as neither unimportant nor extraneous, but as vital components of our Christian lives. Knowing God is our highest priority, but this pursuit should not replace or diminish our interpersonal relationships with others. Rather, our personal interaction with God should produce within us the qualities of character that build and sustain all our relationships.

When offense arises, it is imperative that we practice instant reconciliation. Unresolved conflict can only cause greater damage to the relationship, and eventually, our own walk with the Lord will suffer similar damage. We must understand that as God forgives us our sins, we must allow His Spirit of reconciliation to rule in our own hearts. As with our Lord, we must love by choice, not circumstance. Evil will always be overcome through love.

Read Matthew 5:23–25, 43–48; 6:14; Mark 11:25; Luke 6:27–36.

Questions:

Is there an offense in your life over which hard feelings remain?

_____

_____

Is there an offense you have committed for which reconciliation has not been sought?

_____

_____

Explain in your own words how unforgiveness can hinder your ministry and personal walk with the Lord.

_____

_____

The Heart of the Gospel

Paul regarded the Corinthians as coworkers in the ministry of reconciliation. Yet Paul understood that if they were not fully reconciled to him as Christ's representative, then they could not fully be reconcilers to others. Certain things and people stood in the way of this reconciliation. Competitors, whom Paul called "false apostles" (2 Corinthians 11:13), were trying to win the hearts of the young Corinthian converts. Paul's statement to the Corinthians was "that God was in Christ reconciling the world to Himself, not imputing their trespasses to them, and has committed to us the word of reconciliation" (2 Corinthians 5:19). The very heart of the gospel is reaching out to reconcile others to God, not condemning them or attacking them, but winning them in love.

Word Wealth—*Reconciled*

Reconciled: Greek *katallasso* (kat-al-las'-so); Strong's *#2644*: Means "to change, exchange, reestablish, restore relationships, to make things right, remove an enmity. Five times the word refers to God's reconciling us to Himself through the life, death, and Resurrection of His Son, Jesus (as in Romans 5:10; 2 Corinthians 5:18). Whether speaking of God and man or between believers, *katallasso* describes the reestablishing of a proper loving relationship, which has been broken or disrupted.

In examining the word *reconciled*, we gain a rich understanding of what real ministry is all about. In your own words, explain how the following terms relate to the quality of ministry that Jesus Christ wants us to have.

Change

_____

Reestablish relationships

_____

Restore relationships

_____

Make things right

_____

Remove enmity

_____

Kingdom Life—*Minister Peace*

Jesus prioritized the ministry of human reconciliation with His statement in Matthew 5:9: "Blessed are the peacemakers, for they shall be called sons of God." Jesus made it clear that peacemaking is the birthright and birth assignment of God's sons and daughters.

Peace is often hard-won. It came at great cost to Jesus, who sacrificed His life that we might have peace. A peacemaker is often willing to give up his perceived rights as he pursues the path of seeking and advancing harmony among other individuals, families, and nations, so that they may experience peace through God's love. We can become that kind of peacemaker if we are willing to walk in step with Him and allow the Holy Spirit to empower us and pour the love of God into our hearts.

Read Isaiah 53:5; Romans 12:18.

Questions:

How do you understand Jesus' provision for us in the phrase "chastisement for our peace" (Isaiah 53:5)?

✎ _____

_____

How might we live out this provision in daily life?

✎ _____

_____

What might be the outcome if you minister to others from a heart filled with discord and strife?

✎ _____

_____

Genuine Ministry

The heartbeat of all genuine and authentic ministry is the love of Christ. His love for us motivated Him to die for us. That love should motivate us, should leave us no other option but to respond to others with the same degree of commitment. We love because He first loved us. We give because He gave all.

We should be gripped and consumed by the love of Christ for others. Ministry is not about trying to build a career, attempting to authenticate oneself, or trying to establish a reputation. Our hearts should be on fire and consumed with a passionate love for Jesus Christ that compels us to help others.

Read 1 John 2:6–11; 3:16–23.

Questions:

If our motivations are not pure in ministry, in what ways might we expect God to deal with us as a loving heavenly Father?

Examine your own motives for desiring to minister to others. In what ways have impure motivations hampered your ability to minister effectively?

What steps can you take to cleanse your heart of all impure motivations?

Probing the Depths

One of Paul's goals as a spiritual leader was to try to mature the Corinthians' perspective on how to evaluate leadership. The Corinthians had some very worldly notions about what it takes to be a Christian leader. It seems that they formed their opinions about a Christian leader based on an earthly perspective and using worldly standards of judgment.

This same proclivity exists today. Personal charisma, gifted oratory, charm, and worldly stature often seem to outweigh true ministerial call. We, as the Corinthians did, tend to judge the worth of a Christian leader based on the values of culture and not on biblical ones.

The true measure of a leader can be found in the example of Paul. He was totally committed to his call to spread the gospel and establish churches throughout the known world. He lived what he wrote, that "the gifts and the calling of God are irrevocable" (Romans 11:29). His life demonstrated three basic concepts of leadership:

1. He was committed to the goals and spirit of his call (Philippians 3:7–8).
2. He passed on his objectives to his followers (2 Timothy 2:1–2) and bore with all necessary hardship in pursuing that end (2 Corinthians 4:8–11; 11:23–33).
3. He was alert to change. He adapted to cultural, social, and political changes and thus never lost his relevancy (1 Corinthians 9:19–22).

Record Your Thoughts

Questions:

In what ways has this session caused you to understand your personal accountability differently?

✎_____

_____

What characteristics do you see in the ministry of Paul that you find lacking in your own life or ministry?

✎_____

_____

What changes do you see at this point that need to happen for your ministry to become more effective?

✎_____

What changes can you precipitate these changes?

✎_____

_____

SESSION FIVE

Lights in the Darkness

2 Corinthians 6—9

 Kingdom Key—*Glorify God*

Psalm 50:23 Whoever offers praise glorifies Me; and to him who orders his conduct aright I will show the salvation of God.

The entirety of Psalm 50 relates God's power, majesty, and glory, and is summed up in this closing verse. If we leave God out of our lives and live in rebellion, destruction follows. In contrast, the simple road to success is set forth:

1. Offer praise, and we glorify God. The focus of praise is directed toward God, but in His wisdom we are the ultimate beneficiaries.
2. We receive power to order our conduct; thus, our lifestyle comes into obedience to God.
3. Result: We receive a revelation (understanding)—that is, insight into God's salvation. Our praise becomes a vehicle for God to come to us and to minister through us.

Read Matthew 5:16; Galatians 6:14–16.

Questions:

What characteristics would you expect in any ministry that truly glorifies God?

_____

_____

Is praise a constant and real part of your ministry?

_____

_____

What truly constitutes praise?

✎ _____

The World's View

Sadly, an unbelieving world often has a very cynical and jaundiced view of those in ministry. This cynicism is especially heightened among those of the younger generation, who often see Christian ministers as opportunists, fanatics, and money seekers.

Hollywood has contributed to this misconception with its endless films and television specials about corrupt evangelists and psychopathic Christians. The problem is compounded by the media circus surrounding the fall of Christian television personalities and the decidedly anti-Christian slant to much of media coverage. It is heartbreaking that we must concede some have presented themselves as legitimate ministers of the gospel, only to be shown to have manipulated and cheated people who looked to them for hope in desperate circumstances. More heartbreaking still is the fact that a culture of cynicism and mockery of Christian ministers and evangelists has become part of the fabric of life.

It's in this context of cynicism and doubt that today's ministers and evangelists are called to proclaim the truth of Jesus and live out the power of the gospel. Although the apostle Paul did not have to deal with mass media, he did have to deal with the cynicism of a popular culture and those who accused him of being a phony. Paul's integrity and character were attacked, and he responded by calling believers to evaluate him in light of the gospel and example of Jesus. Those set the standard to which we must continue to conform our lives and ministries.

Read Philippians 3:17; 2 Timothy 2:14–26.

Questions:

Would your ministry stand up to the scrutiny Paul invited?

✎ _____

_____

What areas of weakness do you see, and what can you do to strengthen the integrity of your ministry?

✎_____

_____

Spiritual Power

The apostle Paul had a burning desire to proclaim the message of salvation to a lost and dying world. However, he knew that his effectiveness as a minister and a Christian was directly related to his personal integrity. Integrity produces spiritual power in ministry. Paul was attempting to prove to some of the Corinthians why his ministry was an authentic and legitimate ministry. In preaching the gospel Paul did not want his words to have a hollow echo. First of all, Paul sought to be diligently beyond reproach (2 Corinthians 6:3). Second, Paul wanted the Corinthians to know that there was a price to be paid for excellence in ministry. Paul personally endured great hardship and suffering in order to be able to preach the gospel.

Read Colossians 3:12–17.

Questions:

What does excellence in ministry look like?

✎_____

_____

Can this be said of your own service to the kingdom of God?

✎_____

_____

Which of the characteristics listed in this Colossians passage represent an area of struggle in your walk with the Lord?

✎_____

_____

How has this adversely affected your service to the Lord?

_____

_____

_____

_____

Word Wealth—*Fellowship*

Fellowship: Greek *koinonia* (koy-nohn-ee'-ah); Strong's #*2842*: Sharing, unity, close association, partnership, participation, a society, a communion, a fellowship, contributory help, the brotherhood. *Koinonia* is a unity brought about by the Holy Spirit. In *koinonia* the individual shares in common an intimate bond of fellowship with the rest of Christian society. *Koinonia* cements the believers to the Lord Jesus and to each other.

Kingdom Life—*Promote Fellowship*

The words of the apostle Paul should echo in the hearts of all those today who wish to go into a ministry of any kind. He said, "We give no offense in anything, that our ministry may not be blamed" (2 Corinthians 6:3). In every aspect of his life and ministry, Paul was fully conscious of the fact that he was an ambassador for Christ. Even though his critics attempted to attack him personally and discredit his ministry, Paul lived a life that was above reproach. Even though his character and integrity were under attack, Paul responded in a truly Christlike way. Even when criticized and maligned, Paul made every effort to increase understanding and true fellowship. Paul understood how imperative *koinonia* relationship is to the body of Christ.

The apostle Paul knew that, in order to mature, the church at Corinth must further develop *koinonia*. The obstacles to building this committed unity were the influence of false apostles, partnership in pagan worship and rituals, and associations with nonbelievers. Paul understood that as long as these young converts continued to be influenced by nonbelievers, the believers were going to be inhibited in their spiritual growth. Paul was trying to bind the Corinthians more closely to him and to each other so that true Christian fellowship could be created.

Read Acts 2:42; Philippians 2:1–4; 1 John 1:5–7.

Questions:

What examples of a *koinonia* relationship exist in your life?

✐_____

_____

_____

What steps can you take to promote *koinonia* in your local church?

✐_____

_____

_____

How is *koinonia* expressed and promoted in your ministry?

✐_____

_____

_____

Behind the Scenes

Some of the Corinthians, especially some of the more affluent Gentiles, were attending feasts in pagan temples or dining rooms that were connected to temples (1 Corinthians 8—10). These dinners often involved pagan ceremonies and an animal sacrifice dedicated to a pagan deity. Paul warned that participation in any kind of pagan worship was idolatry. One of these pagan temples was the Asklepion, where pagan banquets occurred. Paul warned believers that they could not partake at the table of demons and the table of the Lord at the same time (1 Corinthians 10:21–22).

Although in contemporary society we do not have specifically pagan banquets where animals are sacrificed, we do have cultural activities that would be the modern equivalent of pagan feasts in that these activities make place for demonic activity and idolatry. Certain nightclubs, movies, theatrical productions, parties, and social occasions open the door to demonic bondage. Certainly not all nonreligious social events fit into this category. But the warnings of the apostle Paul apply to modern believers, and in these days of increasing demonic influence in the culture at large, we must discern which activities and relationships are good for people committed to following the Holy Spirit to use for recreation and leisure and which should be avoided.

Read 1 Corinthians 6:12; 10:23; Colossians 3:12–17.

Questions:

What does understanding the term *fellowship* or *koinonia* teach us about the power of our relationships?

_____

_____

_____

What do you think fellowship provides that is essential to maturing the church, along with prayer and Bible study?

_____

_____

_____

Are there activities in which you engage that do not glorify God?

_____

_____

_____

What changes should you make in your life choices in order to more effectively edify the body of Christ?

_____

_____

_____

Kingdom Extra—*You Are the Temple of the Living God* (2 Corinthians 6:14—7:1)

Paul calls the believers in Corinth to holy living. He begins by warning them not to be "unequally yoked together with unbelievers" (2 Corinthians 6:14). The concept comes from Leviticus 19:19, which prohibits yoking different types of animals together. Not only did Paul refer to marriage partnerships as in 1 Corinthians 7:39, where he warned believers not to marry unbelievers, but Paul referred to any intimate partnership with nonbelievers. The reason for this? "What communion has light with darkness? And what accord has Christ with Belial?" (2 Corinthians 6:14–15). The name *Belial* can be translated "the chief of demons, or Satan." Finally, Paul teaches us that as believers we are "the temple of the living God" (6:16).

When believers allow the idolatry of the world to enter into their hearts, they are opening the door for demonic influence and bondage. God wants believers to be cleansed from all "filthiness of the flesh and spirit" (2 Corinthians 7:1) because He wants to set them free and make their lives and ministries fruitful. Holiness produces freedom and releases spiritual power in the lives of believers.

Questions:

What negative result can occur if partnership or fellowship continues between light and darkness?

✎ _____

_____

_____

What kinds of films, social events, parties, and celebrations would amount to the modern equivalent of pagan worship?

✎ _____

_____

_____

How can a believer discern whether the above events would be spiritually safe or not?

✎ _____

_____

In what ways can a believer enter into a wrong partnership with the world?

✎ _____

_____

Identify the kind of things that could be called idolatry in the life of a believer.

How can we as believers "cleanse ourselves from all filthiness of the flesh and spirit" and work at "perfecting holiness" (2 Corinthians 7:1)?

Why is holiness important for Christians?

What is the relationship between holiness and the release of spiritual power?

Probing the Depths

Parents are often called upon to discipline children. It is a necessary but painful act of true love. It is a parent's duty to instruct and train children to know truth and make right, life-promoting choices. But once the discipline is delivered, a loving parent looks forward to the moment when love can be expressed with hugs and affection.

Paul's call from God to lead and teach the Corinthian church bears many of the same dynamics as the parent-child relationship. In 2 Corinthians 7:8–12, Paul refers to the severe letter he sent to the Corinthians following a painful visit. Some identify 1 Corinthians as the severe letter, but it does not seem to fit that description. Others suggest that 2 Corinthians 10—13 fits that description, but no manuscript evidence supports the separation of those chapters from the rest of the Epistle. According to comments in the *New Spirit-Filled Life Bible* on 2 Corinthians 2:5–11, the problem that letter aimed to correct "involved a challenge to Paul's authority as an apostle. The *severe letter* achieved a degree of correction. The rebel who 'caused grief' [v. 5] not merely for Paul, but for the entire church 'to some extent' [v. 5] had been repudiated 'by the majority' [v. 6] (see 2 Corinthians 7:6–13). With their cooperation, Paul is ready 'to forgive and comfort' [v. 7] the offender. To continue to punish him (after he has repented) would damage not only him but the church and Paul's own work, because it would allow 'Satan' to 'take advantage' [v. 11] of the discord in the church. The traditional identification of the offending person with the incestuous man in 1 Corinthians 5:1–5 is possible, but the offense here seems to have been directed particularly at Paul with the charge being grievous, rude conduct, not immorality."

Ministry and Money

Faithfulness and stewardship regarding money is an essential part of all ministry and an extremely important aspect of Christians' lives. The apostle Paul tells us in 1 Timothy 6:10, "The love of money is a root of all kinds of evil." Notice that Paul does not say money is evil, but it is the "love of money" that is evil. In 1 Timothy 3:3 and in Titus 1:7, Christian leaders are warned not to be greedy for money. Dr. Jack Hayford relates the story of a prominent minister who called him in order to be accountable to him in ministry. One of the questions Dr. Hayford asked him was, "How much is your salary?" Dr. Hayford went on to say that a minister of the gospel should receive a fair remuneration for his work but that it should not be excessive. God does not want ministers to be poor and needy; but neither are they supposed to get rich from the ministry.

As ambassadors of Jesus Christ, the things that we do no longer represent us but rather the One we represent, who is the Lord Jesus Christ. Therefore, we should exercise wisdom regarding the clothes we wear, the cars we drive, the homes in which we live, the words we use, and the general conduct of our lives. People are watching Christians and ministers of the gospel to see if our conduct fits that of our Master and Lord.

This does not mean that we cannot have nice clothes, cars, homes, or enjoy life; all of these are gifts of a generous God. But it does mean that we will be held accountable for the choices we make. We must prayerfully consider how other people may perceive our choices and styles and be drawn to, or repelled from, our verbal witness to the gospel.

Pray to God to reveal anything that may be a stumbling block to others. The Lord may tell you to change some things in your life or ask you to do something entirely unexpected. Is it possible that you are failing to make the best of the gifts God has bestowed upon you? We are responsible for being good stewards so it's important to always do the best you can with what you have. Is it possible that your lack of care for yourself or your possessions is causing others to stumble? Remember, as an ambassador, everything you do represents the "kingdom" you are serving.

Read Matthew 6; Luke 10:7.

Questions:

What principles of conduct can you glean from Matthew 6 that should govern your life choices?

How do you understand Luke 10:7?

Does your lifestyle clearly represent the values of the kingdom?

What changes need to happen in order for you to truly represent the kingdom?

✎ _____

_____

Behind the Scenes

We derive general teaching about giving from Paul's direction to the Corinthians about the collection he was taking up from predominantly Gentile churches in Macedonia and Achaia (Romans 15:26) for the poorer Jewish believers in Judea. These Jewish Christians had been severely affected by the famine that occurred during the reign of the emperor Claudius (A.D. 41–54). The offering being taken up among Paul's churches was intended as aid to all these believers in need, and it would have gone mainly toward purchasing food.

Probing the Depths

Paul called on the Corinthian church to give financially to those in need. He teaches that God multiplies the resources of the believer who gives generously. But this abundance is tied to God's own to enable the recipient to be generous in all circumstances. Material blessing and extra income in and of themselves are not signs of God's blessing, nor is the specific act of giving itself praised. Instead, Paul commends generosity as a lifestyle. A cheerful and willing giver is promised that God will continue to provide so they can continue doing good.

One key to spiritual leadership and ministry breakthrough is found in Jesus' call in Luke 6:38 to "give, and it will be given." Financial obstacles tempt us to give up, but God's Word calls us to give away. True ministry always involves coming to terms with our human tendency to clutch things to ourselves, especially material belongings and time. Jesus exemplifies the essence of giving by the sowing of your own life—your own interests. This pathway of yielding up all to Him often calls us to give when we ourselves may be in need. It seems counterproductive, but giving out of our own need is God's way of clearing the avenues for His purposes—ministry and service sent into the earth through us.

Read Luke 21:1–4; Romans 12:4–8.

Questions:

What kind of giving is blessed by God?

_____

_____

_____

In what way is liberality in giving a manifestation of God's grace?

_____

_____

_____

Is this sacrificial attitude a part of your life and ministry?

_____

_____

_____

Kingdom Life—*To Serve as Jesus*

Paul tells us that Jesus "became poor" (2 Corinthians 8:9). The Greek word used here is *ptocheuo,* which means to be destitute, poor as a beggar, reduced to extreme poverty. The word suggests the bottom rung of poverty, a situation wherein one is totally lacking in this world's goods. What exactly His poverty consisted of is debated. Was it His leaving the riches of glory and, in the language of Philippians 2:8, "being found in appearance as a man, He humbled Himself and became obedient to the point of death, even the death of the cross"? Or was His poverty material—being born into a poor family and living among those of lower social classes? One does not exclude the other. Materially, Jesus was not among the poorest of the poor. His father worked a trade, carpentry, which Jesus learned; and during His ministry, Jesus had the financial support of a number of well-off followers who had been healed and touched by Him. Whatever His poverty denotes exactly, Paul's point is that Jesus voluntarily gave up His rightful claim to being honored and served by others and became the servant of others, making them rich through His poverty.

There are times, though rare enough, when the Lord will request that one in His service divest himself of all this world's goods. However, most of us minister in and through fairly comfortable lives. Regardless of the lifestyle in which we live, we are called to follow the example of our Lord and take upon ourselves the humble attitude of a servant, counting others as more important than ourselves.

Read Philippians 2:1–8.

Questions:

Do you ever consider what gain you may receive from ministry?

_____

What truly motivates your service to others?

_____

Kingdom Life—*God Is the Source*

In the world system of economics, the fear of not having enough is a prime motivator. This fear of poverty and lack creates a climate of economic manipulation, the hoarding of resources, the love of money, dishonest and unethical business dealings, and many other social ills. The Christian's relationship to money should never be one of fear. A Christian should see God as the source of all money and resources. A Christian's mind should be renewed by the Word of God, which defeats a poverty mentality.

Instead of fear, the Christian should have faith in God's ability to provide and His demonstrated willingness to replenish the resources of those who give properly—generously and regularly for the good of others and the glory of God. Paul wrote to some of those poor but generous Macedonian Christians, the Philippians, "My God shall supply all your need according to His riches in glory by Christ Jesus" (Philippians 4:19). That affirmation applies only to those who participate in God's economy in the way that Paul encouraged the Corinthians to participate.

Unlike the world's system of economics, God's system is wrapped up in the principle of giving generously and regularly. In addition God has established the law of sowing and reaping. In giving in order to bless others, we discover that we are blessed.

Instead of trying to hold on to and get more for ourselves, God has given us the privilege of sowing seed into the lives of others. This seed may take the form of love, time, prayer, or money. As we seek to give generously toward the needs of others, then God takes care of our needs. This truth is central to all ministry that is effective and offered in the spirit and strength of Jesus.

Record Your Thoughts

Take a moment to review what God is saying to you in 2 Corinthians 8—9.

Questions:

What single understanding or direction for your life stands out to you the most?

_____

_____

_____

What insight does that give into your true motivations in ministry?

_____

_____

_____

What direction does that invite you to take this week?

_____

_____

Write out a critique of your ministry as it now stands and discuss your insights with someone you trust.

_____

_____

_____

_____

SESSION SIX

Overcoming Challenges

2 Corinthians 10:1—11:15

Kingdom Key—*Walk in Humility*

Colossians 3:12 As the elect of God, holy and beloved, put on tender mercies, kindness, humility, meekness, longsuffering.

Conflict in the body of Christ can often escalate to the point of severe trial and even persecution. Because we are only part of the conflict, we often cannot control the working out of the outcome, only our response. We choose how to respond and, by our responses, can be instrumental in restoring peace or in prolonging the trial. It can be extremely difficult to know the right way to respond. How can we be truthful and loving and act in a way that also has the potential of being effective?

All leaders will face opposition and conflict. Paul's response is a worthy case study of a servant-leader who struggled against worldliness in the hearts of the yet-carnal Corinthians and who sought to call them—at times tenderly, at times sternly; always with love—back to the humble Christ who is powerful through what looks like weakness to a worldly mind-set.

Read Romans 12:9–21.

Questions:

Have you experienced conflict and challenges in relationships within the scope of your ministry?

✎ _____

_____

_____

How did you handle the situations?

✎ _____

_____

What was the outcome?

✎ _____

_____

What other Scriptures can you locate that give insight into how to handle conflict in the body of Christ?

✎ _____

_____

The Real Fight

Conflict in the body of Christ may seem to be brother against brother, but we have an Enemy who wishes to divide us and set us against one another. He wages his battle in the mind and so poisons our thinking as to cause us to perceive one another as adversaries. It is imperative that we remember that we do not fight against one another, but against the wiles of an Enemy set upon our destruction. Discord and enmity in the body of Christ severely weaken the ministry and the witness of all its members.

We do not fight against "flesh and blood" (Ephesians 6:12); therefore, weak and worldly weapons will not suffice. We need weapons that are God-empowered. Their purpose is to demolish anything that opposes God's will. In the opening verses of 2 Corinthians, chapter 10, Paul refers specifically to the battleground of the mind. He speaks of arrogance, rebellious ideas and attitudes, and pride. If we wish to defuse the divisive tactics of the Enemy, we must bring every disobedient thought and attitude into line with the revealed will of God as seen in the life and ministry of Jesus Christ.

Read Ephesians 6:10–18; Colossians 3:12–17.

Questions:

What part does choice play in the verses listed above?

✎ _____

_____

What can we learn from this in regard to being ruled by emotions?

Kingdom Life—*Take Every Thought Captive*

Strongholds are first established in the mind; that is why we are to take every thought captive. Behind a stronghold is also a lie—a place of personal bondage where God's Word has been subjugated to any unscriptural idea or personally confused belief that is held to be true. Behind every lie is a fear, and behind every fear is an idol. Idols are established wherever there exists a failure to trust in the provisions of God that are ours through Jesus Christ. Some of the weapons that pull down these strongholds are: God's Word, the blood of the cross, and the name of Jesus. Strongholds are pulled down and confronted and bondage is broken as these spiritual weapons of our warfare are employed.

Read Hebrews 4:12–13; Revelation 12:11; Mark 16:17; Romans 12:1–2.

Questions:

What does it mean to have a renewed mind?

_____

_____

_____

How might your choices affect this transformation process?

_____

Probing the Depths

Spiritual authority is for the benefit of giving to others, not having for oneself. Authentic leaders understand the delicate balance in the exercise of spiritual authority. In Scripture spiritual authority is received from God as a gift; it is not grabbed; it is recognized and may gain the regard of others, but it is not required and then regulated through controls. The words *life* and *edification* characterize the essence of the exercise of true authority for the construction, not destruction, of others. Godly leaders know that God alone is the source of all spiritual authority and that their authority is a sacred entrustment, never to be used for personal gain or to control or dominate others. Further, a distinct accounting before God will be required of all who are given spiritual authority.

Read John 5:27; Luke 10:10–11; Romans 13:1; Hebrews 13:17.

Questions:

How does ministry to the body of Christ put one in a position of spiritual authority?

_____

_____

What does edification mean to you?

_____

_____

_____

Does your ministry edify the body of Christ?

_____

_____

_____

What changes can you make that will enhance your ability to truly give life through your ministry?

_____

_____

_____

 Word Wealth—*Jealousy*

Jealousy: Greek *zelos* (dzay'-loss); Strong's *#2205*: the root of the English word *zeal.* It signifies eagerness, enthusiasm, intense desire, passionate commitment. The word carries both the idea of zeal (2 Corinthians 7:11; 9:2; Philippians 3:6) and jealousy (Acts 5:17; Romans 13:13).

Godly Jealousy

In 2 Corinthians 11:2, we see Paul's heart revealed. Paul feels "godly jealousy" for the Corinthians. He uses the Old Testament metaphor of Israel as bride and God as Bridegroom (Isaiah 50:1; 54:1–6; Hosea 1—3). In the New Testament Jesus Christ is the Bridegroom and the church is the bride of Christ (Ephesians 5:22–23). Using imagery we find in both Testaments, Paul talks about himself as if he were the father of a bride. In this case Paul is the spiritual father of the Corinthians, who are the bride he wants to present to Christ at His Second Coming. When Paul led the Corinthians to Christ, they became engaged or betrothed to Him.

In contrast to marital engagement in modern secular society, a betrothal in ancient times was an agreement as sacred and binding as marriage itself. The betrothal period was as binding as the marriage itself. Any unfaithfulness on the part of the bride-to-be during this engagement period was considered adultery. In this case Paul is concerned about spiritual adultery and the Corinthians being seduced by "another Jesus," "a different spirit," or "a different gospel" (2 Corinthians 11:4).

Probing the Depths

Second Corinthians shows how certain mind-sets directly oppose the gospel. Have you ever known people who were ready to fight for pure doctrine, but whose spirit was critical toward others, self-centered, and ungracious? (See James 3—4 for an extended description of just such people—doctrinally straight, yet spiritually crooked because of proud self-will not submitted to Christ.) These practice serious error—errors of spirit more than of formal doctrine. This kind of error is quite different from the clear-cut doctrinal error that Paul opposed in his letter to the Galatians, yet it may be more dangerous because we easily overlook it while flourishing our doctrinal swords when defending the faith.

The Corinthians held many harmful mind-sets, including wrong requirements for an apostle and an unhealthy view of spiritual leadership. Led on by latecomer "apostles," the Corinthians judged Paul to be incompetent. They cited: questionable character (vacillation in travel plans, weak personal presence contrasted with strong letters, suspicious handling of charitable funds), lack of references, lack of eloquence in preaching, lack of social standing, and lack of manifestations of the Spirit in his ministry.

Their evaluation was in error. The facts bore witness to the truth. Paul's word was good, although he would change his plans when the situation justified it. He was not a flatterer or wimp. He had felt intimidated by the cultural elitism of Greco-Roman Corinth when he established the church (1 Corinthians 2:1–3), and he preferred to resolve conflicts at the lowest level possible. But he would be as tough as the ministry mission required. The extent to which he endangered himself in his missionary journeys proved that. Accusations of mishandling funds were baseless. On the contrary, the collection was being handled by representatives from each contributing church so there would be no question of impropriety.

The critics appear to be right on one point: Paul was not a trained orator; he lacked the dramatic presentation that training produced, and he admitted it. But substance was more important than style, and the Corinthians' own changed lives were all the expert recommendation he needed and proof enough that Paul had spiritual substance.

The critics were most wrong in what they assumed about Spirit-filled leadership. They minimized the difference between life and leadership in culturally sophisticated but fully pagan Corinth, and life and leadership in the new community established by Jesus—where the greatest is the least, where the leaders voluntarily take the position of servanthood. The greatest error of Paul's critics lay in their worldly views of power. With their job description Paul came out a loser, but Jesus would have as well.

In 1 Corinthians Paul dealt with the faulty focus of the Corinthians. He attempted to center them on the power of the cross, but they preferred the power of the resurrection only. They wanted to know Jesus only as the risen, ascended, exalted One. They had no interest in knowing Jesus also as the crucified One. For them the cross was merely one moment in the life and ministry of Jesus. They agreed that He died "for our sins" (1 Corinthians 15:3), but the cross had no other meaning for Christian life. What mattered were experiences of resurrection power—signs and wonders, miracles, tongues, visions, and all kinds of exciting spiritual experiences.

The Corinthians distorted the meaning of spiritual manifestations.

They assigned to them too much value while at the same time giving no value to the manifestations of cross power—sacrificial patience, humility, endurance, and costly love that "suffers long and is kind; . . . does not envy; . . . does not parade itself, is not puffed up; does not behave rudely" (1 Corinthians 13:4–5). These manifestations of God's power shine through the ministry of Jesus and most brightly in His voluntary submission to the cross. In 2 Corinthians Paul makes multiple attempts to help the erring Corinthians see and value these dimensions of God's power as much as the signs and wonders.

Signs-and-wonders power is visible even to carnal people, and it is tempting to desire such self-evident power simply for selfish purposes. One mark of carnal Christians is their self-will, their grasping for power that they may use for themselves. This self-centeredness is manifested in their judgmental, unloving spirits, their impatience with those who do not always agree with them, their arrogance and insensitivity toward others. Truly Spirit-filled, Spirit-directed believers live a life of both the cross and the resurrection: The life of the cross is manifested in their being crucified to their flesh and to the world. This is the continuing role of Christ's cross in the Spirit-filled life, the cross He calls us to take up as we follow Him. Resurrection life is manifested in the things we typically call supernatural—signs, wonders, miracles, and so forth.

The carnal Corinthians who opposed Paul sought and acknowledged only those dimensions of divine power that appealed to them. They were enthralled with resurrection-like manifestations of God's power, and they discounted and despised all others. Humility, gentleness, hardship, endurance, patience—these struck them as things either to be avoided or of no merit, certainly not as manifestations of God's power. They judged leaders only on the single criterion of how well they manifested signs and wonders in their ministries. Although Paul manifested that kind of power, it was not enough for the Corinthians and less than the power displayed by the newcomer leaders who sought acceptance by the Corinthians.

The Corinthians' harmful view of ministry distorted the gospel by diminishing the importance of the cross. It also limited the ongoing experience of the gospel to only sensational experiences. This diluted gospel would never bear the fruit of the Spirit; it could not create a community of loving, sacrificial believers. Genuine gospel leaders were rejected in favor of flesh-pleasing performers. Finally, rejecting Jesus crucified in favor of only Jesus glorified flirts with idolatry—remaking God in our image, an image that appeals to our preferences and contains nothing to challenge our sinfulness.

Read 2 Corinthians 11:1–15; 5:7.

Questions:

What opinions and choices of today's world seem to mimic the attitude of the Corinthians?

_____

_____

What can be learned from Paul's actions and words that may be of value in confronting similar distortions of the gospel today?

_____

_____

What part do "signs and wonders" (2 Corinthians 12:12) play in your own life and ministry?

_____

_____

Do you "walk by faith" or by "sight" (2 Corinthians 5:7) in your own ministry?

_____

_____

Behind the Scenes

In order to understand 2 Corinthians 11:5–13, it is necessary to understand the ancient Greco-Roman practice of patronage relationships. As strange as it may seem to us, some at Corinth (probably opponents and the Corinthians sympathetic to them) accused Paul of not being a true apostle of God because he did not accept contributions from Corinth. Earlier, when he wrote 1 Corinthians, Paul acknowledged that the Lord "commanded that those who preach the gospel should live from the gospel" (1 Corinthians 9:14). Yet he exempted himself from this command so that he could "present the gospel of Christ without charge" (1 Corinthians 9:18). Rather than see Paul's self-support as desirable, some Corinthians were insulted by Paul's refusal to accept their gift. The reason? To Paul preaching the gospel free of charge kept him free of any obligations to special interests within the local congregation. He wanted to be the benefactor of the church, to be the father who willingly gave of himself to his spiritual children, not expecting to be repaid. But some of the Corinthians wanted to match Paul's gift of the gospel at no charge with their own gift. Apparently, they felt that not matching his gift with their own gift would leave them in a position of being Paul's social inferiors. This feeling makes sense when we understand the social context of friendship and gift-giving and gift-receiving.

In ancient Corinth there were a variety of social relationships or friendships between people of different social status. A benefactor or patron would give money and other material benefits and expect to receive honor, praise, and other things in return. The recipients of these gifts would automatically be put in a socially inferior role—obliged either to assert their equality by a corresponding gift of the same or greater value or to accept their role as one who owed expressions of honor to their patron.

Paul's opponents used his refusal to accept support as proof that he was not a legitimate apostle. They argued that if he were a true apostle, he would have been worthy of such support and would have taken it, as any respectable teacher of the day would accept tuition from students.

Record Your Thoughts

This lesson includes one of the most important references to spiritual warfare in the New Testament, 2 Corinthians 10:3–5.

Questions:

How does what you have learned in this lesson shed any new light on your understanding of "strongholds," "arguments" that exalt themselves against God, and "thoughts" disobedient to Christ?

✎ _____

_____

_____

How has this lesson affected your understanding of the worldliness the church must combat?

✎ _____

_____

_____

What impresses you the most about Paul's situation with the Corinthians?

✎ _____

_____

_____

In what ways have you perhaps been applying worldly views to your life in Christ and within His church?

✎ _____

_____

_____

In what way does the cross correct those worldly views?

✎ _____

_____

_____

How does God want you to tear down such strongholds and make such thoughts obedient to Christ?

✎ _____

_____

_____

_____

SESSION SEVEN

The Paradox of Ministry

2 Corinthians 11:16—12:9

Kingdom Key—Decrease into Greatness

Philippians 2:3 Let nothing be done through selfish ambition or conceit, but in lowliness of mind let each esteem others better than himself.

Paradoxes, as used in Scripture, are pregnant with meaning, but they can truly challenge our minds. They present us with truths that appear to have no way of being true and are totally alien to our experience. Paradoxes seem to contradict themselves.

The life of Paul seemed to be nearly defined by paradox. Though apparently weak in the socially accepted attributes of a leader, Paul's words comprise a huge part of the New Testament. He brought wholeness and healing to countless believers, yet he suffered with an affliction throughout his entire ministry. He is a great example of faith to millions, yet he lived as an itinerant servant, often lacking in the necessities of life.

We learn from Paul that if you want to be truly great, then the direction you must go is down. You must descend into greatness. At the heart of this paradox is still another paradox: Greatness is not a measure of self-will, but rather self-abandonment. The more you lose, the more you gain.

Read Luke 22:24–30; Ephesians 5:21–33; 6:5–9; Matthew 6:19–21; Luke 12:13–34; 1 Timothy 6:17–19.

Question:

What are some other examples of paradoxes in kingdom living?

_____

_____

Boast in the Lord

Paul found himself in an unwanted competition that required him to boast. He had been compared unfavorably against late-coming "apostles" who wanted the Corinthians to embrace them as their spiritual leaders. They had presented impressive résumés, complete with sterling recommendations from other leaders, and their in-person performances (they called it "ministry") pleased influential members of this congregation in Greece's entertainment capital. If a vote had been taken, it looked sure that Paul would be defeated and turned out of office as the official apostle of Christ to Corinth.

Paul had another problem: He found boasting not only distasteful but insulting to God. As he said in 2 Corinthians 10:17, all glorying (or boasting) is to be done only "in the LORD." That is, the only boasting any of us should do is boasting of our Lord and His achievements. If only the Corinthians and the false apostles had seen the power of God in the cross and boasted in it, then they would have seen the fullness of God's power at work in Paul and would have been reconciled to him. But because they were not reconciled, Paul was compelled to respond to the boasting competition.

Read Psalms 34:2–3; 94:4; Proverbs 27:1–2; Romans 11:15–18; Galatians 6:14; Ephesians 2:8–9.

Questions:

What does it mean to boast in the Lord?

_____

_____

What do you see as the root cause of self-boasting?

_____

_____

In what ways might self-assertion inhibit or damage ministry?

_____

_____

_____

Behind the Scenes

It is difficult for contemporary Christians to understand Paul's references to boasting in light of the Bible's emphasis on such things as humility and the need not to be prideful. However, self-admiration and self-praise were the custom in Greco-Roman society as a means of building status. As the entertainment capital of Greece, Corinth hosted numerous games and oratory contests. Orators and debaters, who held the place that actors and rock groups do in our society today, came from around the ancient world to perform in Corinth's 14,000-seat theater. These masters of debate and rhetoric would often wear impressive clothing and jewelry and have elaborate hairstyles.

The popular teachers and philosophers of the day used self-praise to develop a following and gain social power. Ancient authors Cicero and Plutarch wrote rules on the art of self-praise. In addition the Sophists, orators who practiced an extremely showy form of oratory, developed a whole approach to self-praise and boasting in their rhetoric. In 2 Corinthians 10—13, Paul is specifically attacking those who were using the sophistic method of evaluating people and their public speaking skills. The criticism that Paul was not an effective speaker probably means that he did not use the techniques of the Sophists in his preaching and teaching. Judged by their oratorical theatrics, he came off as untrained. But apart from training in their methods, Paul also resisted the content of their speeches, especially the speech of self-recommendation. Yet at this point in 2 Corinthians, he is so concerned about the inroads these false apostles have made, that he feels he must take them on directly and show their emptiness.

The Fool's Speech

Some of the Corinthians looked down on Paul and found him weak and foolish. Paul considered the boasting "according to the flesh" (2 Corinthians 11:18) of their false apostles foolish. Yet, for the sake of the Corinthians, Paul was willing to be thought foolish and do things he himself regarded as foolish.

Many Bible students have labeled 2 Corinthians 11:22—12:10 "The Fool's Speech" because it seems to be Paul's carefully crafted response to speeches of self-recommendation given by the false apostles at Corinth. In the Greco-Roman world, the speech to praise a person was called an encomium. It followed a traditional pattern by informing the listener of: place of origin, education, special intellectual pursuits, virtues, deeds, blessings and/or endowments, and a self-honoring memorial. Look up these verses in 2 Corinthians to discover how Paul's response relates to the original speech pattern we believe his opponents followed.

 Kingdom Life—*It's All About Jesus*

A spirit of boasting, even over spiritual accomplishments, will create separation between those who boast of their accomplishments and those who do not. Those who boast in such things will not want to identify with those they think are less spiritual than they. In fact, as 2 Corinthians 11:19–20 shows, rather than identify pastorally with those less spiritual or less mature than they, Paul's opponents acted out their prideful arrogance in abusing the Corinthians. In stark contrast, rather than boasting of his strength and looking with contempt on those who were weak, Paul identified with them in their hurt.

Paul's boasting is confined to an unnamed man who went up to the third heaven without knowledge of his state (in or out of the body) and who saw and heard things he could not tell! It is commonly understood that Paul speaks of himself in this passage; however, he speaks with reserve to avoid boasting about himself rather than boasting in the Lord, who granted such a privilege.

From all we know about the Corinthians, it is plausible that some of them valued "visions and revelations of the Lord" (2 Corinthians 12:1) highly and that Paul's opponents made much about these supernatural communications as, again, evidence of their superior apostleship. To the extent that people decided such visions and revelations made Paul's opponents more spiritual than Paul, those who trusted them were trusting assertions that could not be verified. However, Paul invited the Corinthians to judge him according to what they could see and hear. He was confident that the life of Jesus within would outshine anything of the world.

Read 1 John 5:4–5.

Questions:

What does it mean to "overcome the world" (1 John 5:4)?

In what ways can actions and behavior equate to boasting?

_____

_____

How does worldly boasting diminish the lordship of Jesus?

_____

Behind the Scenes

In reading 2 Corinthians 11:32–33, one may wonder why Paul chose this particular point in his letter to mention a seemingly unrelated situation. However, there is significant symbolic inference in Paul's reference to his escape from King Aretas.

The Roman army had many customs and rituals surrounding battle and conquest. One such custom involved the reward for the first soldier to breach the wall of an opposing city. The first soldier to reach the top of a protective wall received a crown known as the *corona muralis.* This crown was made of gold and was one of the highest possible honors of a Roman soldier. It was never awarded to any soldier until the claim of being first to scale the wall was verified following a stringent investigation.

Question:

With this in mind, what was Paul communicating to the Corinthians by recounting his escape?

_____

Probing the Depths

Paul's "thorn in the flesh" (2 Corinthians 12:7) and his three unmet requests for its removal give us insight into how we should react in similar, seemingly unchangeable situations.

Because of some ambiguities, it seems very unwise to form dogmatic conclusions about certain particulars of this section. What is clear, however, is a "thorn in the flesh" (an intense, wearying difficulty or affliction) had come by means of a "messenger of Satan" (probably a demonically instigated assault). God's providence clearly allowed this (grammatically, a "divine passive," indicating God as the unseen Agent overseeing the entire process) that Paul might avoid being "exalted above measure by the abundance of the revelations" (12:7).

Though it is futile to try to identify the "thorn," it caused Paul great consternation and ultimately served a good purpose, becoming the occasion for a revelation to him of the overcoming grace of God, which proved "sufficient" (v. 9) in the midst of Paul's "weakness" (v. 9).

We must also note that though God does not respond to Paul's repeated pleading "that it might depart from" (v. 8) him by removing it, there is no indication God is upset with Paul for so pleading. In fact God's answer indicates His concern to respond, even though the outcome is different from the one Paul requested. (Nor does Paul's repeated praying without receiving the answer he wanted show that he lacked faith. This passage emphasizes God's sovereignty in answering the apostle whose faith we often think of as looming larger than life, especially in the descriptions of signs and wonders that accompanied his ministry, according to Acts.)

Finally, it is important to note that God's answer was not seen by Paul as punitive; nor did it cause him to resign himself to buffeting with a defeatist attitude. Rather, it affirmed in Paul that whenever Satan buffets him (either directly as the destructive adversary or indirectly as God's controlled agent to bring about character development), he can "boast in" his "infirmities" because Jesus' "grace" and "strength" will be "sufficient" (2 Corinthians 12:9) to enable him to continue in his apostolic ministry. Neither the thorn, any messenger of Satan, nor any character-refining test from God will cause him to cease serving God. He can therefore "take pleasure . . . for when" he is personally "weak, then" he can be "strong" in Jesus (v. 10).

Read Matthew 10:37–39; Acts 17:28; Romans 8:28; Philippians 4:13.

Questions:

What do these Scripture portions tell you regarding the focus of ministry?

✎ _____

_____

Have you experienced unanswered prayer in your walk with the Lord?

✎_____

_____

What effect has this had on your life and ministry?

✎_____

_____

How do you now see those unanswered prayers?

✎_____

_____

Word Wealth—*Grace*

Grace: Greek *charis* (khar'-ece); Strong's #*5485*: From the same root as *chara*, meaning "joy," and *chairo*, which means "to rejoice." *Charis* causes rejoicing. It is the word for God's grace as extended to sinful man. It signifies unmerited favor, undeserved blessing, and a free gift. Additionally, grace refers to God's motivating believers to desire and do His will, to His enabling them with both power and endurance to persevere in doing His will.

The mystery of the gospel of Jesus Christ and the secret of all ministry is wrapped up in the word *grace*.

Read John 1:14–17; 1 Corinthians 15:10; Ephesians 1:3–14; Philippians 2:13.

Questions:

Is God's grace a focal point of your kingdom walk and your ministry?

✎_____

_____

How might others learn of God's grace through your life?

✎_____

_____

Record Your Thoughts
Questions:

In what ways do you see God's power expressed in the cross of Christ?

_____

_____

_____

How was God's power expressed in Paul's hardships, including his thorn in the flesh?

_____

_____

_____

How in your life can you see God's power expressed through your weaknesses or "infirmities" (2 Corinthians 12:5, 9)?

_____

_____

_____

How do your ministry priorities compare to those of Paul?

_____

_____

_____

What do you feel the need to understand more fully from this portion of Scripture?

_____

_____

Based on what you do understand, what changes in your perspective on ministry or your actions in ministry does this portion of Scripture direct you to make?

_____

_____

SESSION EIGHT

Spirit-Filled Ministry

2 Corinthians 12:10—13:14

Kingdom Key—*Be Enabled*

Acts 1:8 You shall receive power when the Holy Spirit has come upon you; and you shall be witnesses to Me in Jerusalem, and in all Judea and Samaria, and to the end of the earth.

What enabled the early disciples and followers of Jesus Christ to turn the world upside down was not their affluence, education, or exceptional human abilities. These were ordinary people whose lives were dramatically changed through a personal encounter with Jesus Christ. In the same way today, when our lives are dramatically changed by Jesus Christ by the power of the Holy Spirit, we are able to become instruments of power that can transform the lives of others.

Read Acts 4:30; 5:12; 6:8; 14:3; 15:12; 1 Corinthians 4:20; 12:6–11; Ephesians 3:14–21.

Questions:

What is the purpose of the "power that works in us" (Ephesians 3:20)?

Do signs and wonders follow your ministry?

Why do you believe this is so?

Kingdom Life—*Minister in Power*

Although Paul did not like to boast about himself or "strut his stuff," he moved boldly in the supernatural gifts of the Holy Spirit when God directed him to do so. Paul was not preaching a merely intellectual gospel. Paul's ministry included "signs and wonders and mighty deeds" (2 Corinthians 12:12).

In the ministry of Jesus Christ, the apostles, and in the lives of believers today, there should be a supernatural element to the proclamation of the gospel. Yet, according to Paul, the signs of a true apostle go beyond miracles. The miracles that God worked through Paul were done in the context of suffering, endurance, faithfulness in doctrinal matters, moral purity, accountability, and integrity of heart.

Read Matthew 7:21–27; 1 Corinthians 13; 2 Peter 1:2–8.

Question:

How would you describe the heart attitudes and motives of one through whom the Spirit manifests signs and wonders?

_____

Probing the Depths

Paul did not emphasize "signs and wonders and mighty deeds" (2 Corinthians 12:12) in his ministry as his opponents apparently did. What many would list first in an assertion of spiritual authority, Paul mentioned last and did not elaborate, since the Corinthians had witnessed them. Paul's opponents would have made much more of such spiritual manifestations, although it is questionable whether or not the Corinthians had themselves witnessed such manifestations through the opponents. Because the opponents relied so much on the recommendation of others and on their own self-recommendation, it is likely that they reported more signs and wonders than the Corinthians actually witnessed firsthand (12:6). In addition, the unhealthy, imbalanced exaltation of signs and wonders by some Corinthians caused Paul to de-emphasize them in order to help this church find balance.

Although the saying is often overused and little understood, it remains unchangingly true: "Don't seek the gifts; seek the Giver of the gifts." Putting God's kingdom first is the first step on the pathway of God's miracles, and you cannot walk this pathway unless determining His will, purpose, and glory is your first priority as you pursue His call on your life. Seeking first the signs and wonders is indicative of one seeking instant relief of trial, the thrill of the supernatural, and the freedom of responsibility or consequence.

Read Matthew 6:25–34; 2 Timothy 1:6–14.

Questions:

What heart attitude leads to a life free of concern about tomorrow?

_____

_____

How can putting God's kingdom first result in a life free of worry and fear?

_____

_____

How can worry and anxiety negatively affect the flow of the Spirit in the life of a believer?

_____

_____

Why do you believe Paul linked "power," "love," and a "sound mind" (2 Timothy 1:7) in speaking to Timothy of ministry?

_____

_____

Behind the Scenes

The Corinthians had some pretty worldly ideas in assessing leadership. Their ideas about power and authority came from the surrounding pagan culture and were not truly biblical. One of the reasons the so-called "super apostles" and false teachers were able to get such a foothold in Corinth was because they fit the worldly image of what a strong leader was supposed to be. In short they used false criteria in judging leadership. They were looking for leaders with natural charisma, charm, strong rhetorical skills, and engaging testimonies about their supernatural experiences. Paul spared no effort, including playing the part of a fool, in order to get them to see that genuine spiritual leadership followed the servant-model of Jesus Christ, which emphasized self-sacrifice, humility, and identification with the weak and needy as much as works of power. For Paul, as for Jesus, there was no either-or choice: either works of power or servant-leadership character. Instead, both, in the proper relationship, characterized authentic apostolic leadership.

A spiritual leader must have the right motives in leadership. The apostle Paul was never self-serving. His constant desire was to please God and serve His church. God could trust him with a difficult and important ministry.

Kingdom Life—*Walk in Authentic Faith*

Authentic faith is founded on the promises of God as found in His Word; it is not presumptuous. Presumptuous ideas about faith lead to attitudinal or behavioral sin, to missing the mark of faith's true meaning. Presumptuous attitudes are present when, in the name of faith, a person either thinks faith is wishful thinking or a fanciful attitude, assuming God should relieve all their discomfort and jump to their requests— or they reject any responsibility of their own for offering a devoted heart and the commitment to serve Him regardless of their life condition. Presumption desires the promise of God without living a life for God and is hypocritical in His sight.

To protect from a presumptuous attitude, you must first root your faith in what God in Christ has provided through His redemption, not on what you might gain. You must develop your own vibrant, personal relationship with the Lord so that your faith is based on what your heart knows, not on whatever faith or power you may see in the life of another. And finally, you must learn to walk in faith, growing in an intimate relationship with the Author and Finisher of your faith, so that you are known as His and found in Him.

Read Psalms 19:12; 51:7–17; 26:1–3; Proverbs 16:2; 1 Corinthians 4:5; 1 Thessalonians 2:4.

Questions:

Our inner motives in ministry are extremely important to the Lord. How do you think the purity of our motives affects our spiritual authority?

What prayer request in Psalm 19:12 asks God to help us keep our motives pure?

When we humbly walk before the Lord, how does a Holy Spirit–inspired confidence regarding our motives in ministry give us inner strength in facing opposition?

What, if anything, do you need to do to cleanse your conscience and purify your motives for ministry so that you can serve more effectively and with greater strength in the face of all kinds of opposition?

Probing the Depths

Like modern pastors and spiritual leaders, Paul had to deal with problems in the church. He couldn't ignore them or sweep them under the carpet. In order to be the spiritual leader God called him to be, Paul had to confront the sin in the Corinthian church, discipline the Corinthians spiritually, and exhort them to live pure and holy lives. Like many of our churches today, the Corinthians had allowed the corrupt values and practices of the surrounding pagan culture to pollute their lives. Paul was zealous to see spiritual health restored to the church at Corinth, and he knew this could happen only if the people repented of their sins and allowed the Holy Spirit to sanctify them.

When Christians have received much blessing and enlightenment from God and then turn their backs on Him, it is an extremely serious matter. Privileges do not protect us either from responsibility or from discipline. They increase our responsibility and our culpability and deserve more serious discipline. This is particularly true of church leaders.

Church discipline can be a very controversial issue. We learn through Paul's ministry that Christians who turn their backs on God should undergo some discipline in their home church. However, the main purpose of discipline is not retribution but restoration. Even though we are not retributively punished for our sins, God will sometimes allow us to suffer when we have sinned in order to restore us to fellowship with Him. This discipline from God may come in the form of loving correction from those God has placed in authority over us in our local church. We need to submit to what God is doing and attempt to learn from the experience. If it is God's discipline, it will last as long as is necessary. There is no quick-fix solution to some of these problems and no easy way out. Discipline will direct us to God, drive us to prayer, and bring us into submission to Him.

Read 1 Corinthians 12:12–26. We are all one in the Lord. We need to remember this when discipline is called for.

Questions:

What should be the core motivation for church discipline?

_____

_____

When a brother or sister is in sin, what is the effect on the body of Christ?

_____

_____

What gives church leaders the right and responsibility to discipline those under their authority?

_____

Word Wealth—*Complete*

Complete: Greek *katartisis* (kat-ar'-tis-is); Strong's *#2676*: Related to the verb *katartizo*, which is used in Matthew 4:21 for the mending of the disciples' fishing nets. When used of humans, it includes the idea of making repairs or the necessary adjustments to bring one to full health, usefulness, or integrity. Helping one become complete involves the actions of equipping, disciplining, training, and improving.

The Essence of Ministry

In 2 Corinthians 13:3–9, Paul sums up the essence of ministering in the Spirit and strength of Jesus. In order to effectively minister to others, you must recognize that the ability and power to minister come from God alone. You must embrace the truth that God's strength is perfected in your weakness. This truth will set you free to be used powerfully by God.

Of even greater importance, it is imperative that one who ministers to the body of Christ be compelled by the love of Christ. That love will unfailingly focus outwardly, toward the kingdom and people of God. Ministry that is motivated by love will not seek its own but will encourage, edify, and uphold those whom Christ loves.

Record Your Thoughts

Allow the Lord to speak to you about what He may want to change or resurrect in your life. Allow yourself to experience a freeing transformation. Surrender your life with its plans, purposes, and pursuits into His hands, not out of fear or some sense of morbidity, but with the trusting confidence a young child has toward his loving father. Expect that when you release your life to Him, that He will bless you and purify your desires. Expect that God will reveal to you His blessing and goodness, even though He may require some changes.

Questions:

In what areas is the Holy Spirit asking you to die to your own desires, dreams, goals, or plans?

✎ _____

_____

_____

What do you feel are God's desires for you?

✎ _____

_____

What do you believe are God's goals for you?

✎_____

_____

_____

_____

What do you believe are God's dreams for you?

✎_____

_____

_____

_____

What do you believe are God's plans for your life and ministry?

✎_____

_____

_____

_____

Spend some time rejoicing in what God has revealed to you. Then act upon what God has said to you in faith, fully expecting His miracle provision, guidance, and blessing. Whether you are a layperson or a vocational minister, remember the words of Paul when he said, "Fulfill your ministry" (2 Timothy 4:5).

Do not allow what the Lord has told you to dissipate. Write down specific things the Lord has told you to do. Let these things be an action plan from God to you. Write them down in a place where you can review them regularly and act on each one of them.

✎_____

_____

_____

_____

_____

SESSION NINE

Prepared to Lead
1 Timothy 1—3

Kingdom Key—*Be Diligent*

2 Peter 1:5–7 For this very reason, giving all diligence, add to your faith virtue, to virtue knowledge, to knowledge self-control, to self-control perseverance, to perseverance godliness, to godliness brotherly kindness, and to brotherly kindness love.

Paul's first letter to Timothy not only gave guidance in fulfilling responsibilities as a church leader and minister to the body of Christ, but it has been a handbook for those who will minister throughout the church age. A clear lesson gleaned from Paul's instructions is that the church must have well-trained, deeply devoted, and highly consecrated ministry. Furthermore, ministers must stay in constant touch with God through prayer and study of the Bible. Those who would minister must first nourish their own souls in the words of faith and good doctrine and then teach the people the essentials of the faith. Diligently practicing godliness in his own conduct, the minister must encourage others to do the same.

Read Matthew 7:15–23; 24:24; Philippians 2:12–16.

Questions:

How is spiritual deception possible in the church?

_____

_____

How can this be prevented?

_____

_____

In what way is love at the root of ensuring sound doctrine in your ministry?

_____

_____

Behind the Scenes

The books of 1 Timothy, 2 Timothy, and Titus are often referred to as the "Pastoral Epistles." Paul wrote these books to two of his spiritual sons, Timothy (who was pastor of the church in Ephesus), and Titus (who was responsible for the church on the island of Crete).

The primary purpose of 1 Timothy was to encourage Timothy in his difficult job of dealing with false doctrine as well as to give instruction concerning his role as pastor and church leader.

Many Bible scholars believe that this epistle was written after Paul's first Roman imprisonment. After his release from prison, Paul ministered for a number of years and then was arrested again when the emperor Nero began to launch persecution against the church. Finally, Paul was executed for his bold stand for Jesus Christ—possibly by being beheaded. The events in the Pastoral Epistles took place during this period of freedom between Paul's two imprisonments. The apostle Paul maintained a vibrant faith in the midst of severe trial, persecution, imprisonment, and eventually martyrdom.

Word Wealth—*Pastor*

Pastor: Hebrew *ra'ah* (rah-'ah); Strong's #7462: Actually a verb, although in current thought it would seem to be a noun in referring to the leader of a local church. Action is inherent in the meaning of this ancient Hebrew word. It actually means to lead, shepherd, feed, care for, and associate with as a friend.

Probing the Depths

When Paul talked about "fables and endless genealogies" (1 Timothy 1:4), he was talking about the ancient practice of inventing romantic and fictitious tales tracing the historical background of cities and families back to the gods. The ancient world was fascinated with genealogies. Men like Alexander the Great paid to have a pedigree constructed tracing forefathers back to mythological gods. The ideas that gave birth to full-blown Gnosticism in the second century were influential in Paul's time, including fables and genealogies.

The real danger of Gnostic ideas lay in their promotion of two very dangerous false beliefs: that matter and the body are evil, and only nonmaterial spirit is good. Ironically, this false teaching produced two opposite types of behavior: a libertinism ("all things are permissible") and a false asceticism ("touch not, handle not"). Some Gnostics forbade people to marry and advocated strict dietary laws. These taught that a person should completely deny his or her body through harsh and rigorous self-denial and discipline. Since the Gnostics taught that the body did not ultimately matter, others took this idea as a license to indulge in complete immorality.

Both of these ideas are unbiblical and can cause serious spiritual harm. Many of the Gnostic ideas are found in what is called the New Age movement, mysticism, and the cults. In addition Gnostic, heretical ideas have been introduced into some areas of the church. Excessive legalism, with its long lists of dos and don'ts and an inordinate emphasis on fleshly means to place the body under subjection, can be Gnostic. Also Gnostic are forms of "superspirituality" in which visions, dreams, and ecstatic supernatural experiences are prized, while the ordinary responsibilities of life are despised. Such false spirituality pits the supernatural against the natural, God's good creation against God's redemption, and being spiritual against being human. It undercuts itself, devalues creation, and leaves little to be redeemed.

Question:

What are some examples of modern spiritual error or current unbalanced teachings that may have been influenced by Gnostic thought?

Kingdom Life—*Avoid Deception*

Wise believers do not allow themselves to become distracted from their devotion by extraneous arguments and legends that lead one away from Scripture. Realizing that truth is more practice than theory, judge all teaching by what it produces, not by how it sounds. You must guard carefully the truth you have been taught—truth that is biblical and God-breathed. Reject all human knowledge that denies the faith. Avoid the deception of demonically inspired teachings that sound good but bring destruction and death in the end.

Read Luke 6:43–49; James 1:21–27.

Questions:

How can true teachings be identified?

_____

What one element is present in all valid kingdom ministry?

_____

How can you guard against being misled or promoting unsound doctrine?

_____

Other than in words, in what ways does your ministry to the body of Christ proclaim truth?

_____

Probing the Depths

One of the tasks of a Christian leader is to teach "sound doctrine" (1 Timothy 1:10). In order to teach sound doctrine, pastors, Bible teachers, and other Christian leaders must recognize the full inerrant authority of the Bible and live under the full authority of the Bible in every area of life. Sadly, there has been an attempt to undermine the authority and inerrancy of Scripture within the evangelical community. The result has been an attempt to accommodate the Scriptures to the world spirit of this age and the philosophies and belief systems that are currently fashionable.

When the church begins to violate Paul's admonishment to "teach no other doctrine" (1 Timothy 1:3), we begin to see the results of such accommodation within the Christian culture. Easy divorce, adultery, theistic evolution (which attempts to mix the theories of Darwin with the Scripture), false teaching, sexual immorality, abortion, and the acceptance of homosexuality are all symptoms of cultural accommodation and a weakened view of Scripture.

 Kingdom Life—*Intercede*

One of the most important ministries of the local church and of individual Christians is the ministry of intercessory prayer. So important is this ministry that Paul starts off his discussion on intercessory prayer with, "I exhort first of all that supplications, prayers, intercessions, and giving of thanks be made for all men" (1 Timothy 2:1). In this passage of Scripture, the church is given the responsibility to intercede and pray for local, state, and federal governmental leaders, the heads of industry, the media, the school systems, the courts, and "all who are in authority" (2:2). Paul is saying that there is a direct relationship between the quality of life in our communities, cities, and nation and the quality of our intercessory prayer life.

Read 2 Chronicles 7:14.

Questions:

What does it mean to humble yourself in prayer?

_____

_____

What is the difference between supplication, prayer, and intercession?

_____

_____

Probing the Depths

In addition to worship, making disciples, teaching the Word, evangelism, and fellowship, one of the key ministries of the local church should be intercessory prayer. In recent times we have seen the Holy Spirit revive this much-needed focus on intercessory prayer. If Christians wish to see good government, the healing of our homes, communities, cities, and nations, then prayer, fasting, and intercessory prayer are the biblical keys. The power of intercessory prayer is that it recognizes that the primary warfare is spiritual and takes place in the invisible realm. Prayer, fasting, and intercessory prayer allow the church to unleash powerful spiritual weapons that have the capacity to effect real change in our world.

Women in the ministry is a hotly debated issue in some quarters of the Christian community. There are some who see Paul's statement, "I do not permit a woman to teach or to have authority over a man, but to be in silence" (1 Timothy 2:12), as a clear prohibition against women in the ministry. But this Scripture must be taken in the greater context of the entire Old and New Testaments. In the Old Testament, some of Israel's finest leaders were women, such as Deborah the judge. Second, in the New Testament, women like Phoebe (Romans 16:1) and Philip's daughters (Acts 21:9) were involved in ministry. In addition, in Philippians 4:2, Syntyche and Euodia appeared to have leadership roles in their fellowships.

Hayford's Bible Handbook says, "It is puzzling why the place of women in ministry is contested by some in the church. Women had an equal place in the Upper Room awaiting the Holy Spirit's coming and the birth of the church (Acts 1:14). Then Peter's prophetic sermon at Pentecost affirmed the Old Testament promise was now realized: 'your daughters' and 'maidservants' would now share fully and equally with men in realizing the anointing, fullness, and ministry of the Holy Spirit, making them effective in witness and service for the spread of the gospel."

For those who might think that this viewpoint is merely an accommodation to the thinking of our contemporary culture, *Hayford's Bible Handbook* adds, "The acceptance of women in a public place of ministry in the church is not a concession to the spirit of the feminist movement. But the refusal of such a place might be a concession to an order of male chauvinism unwarranted by and unsupported in the Scriptures. Clearly, women did speak—preach and prophesy—in the early church."

The *New Spirit-Filled Life Bible* notes that "the prohibition of verse 12 refers to the authoritative office of apostolic teacher in the church. It does not forbid women to educate, proclaim truth, or exhort (prophesy)."

Qualifications of Christian Leaders

In 1 Timothy 3:1–13, Paul outlines the qualities that should characterize any Christian leader. Unlike our secular society, which in many cases is willing to overlook the moral character of a man in a position of leadership, the Bible teaches that there is an inseparable link between a man's moral character and the ability to lead effectively. In addition, the Bible teaches that a Christian leader must be able to manage his own home well (3:4–5, 11–12). How a man treats his wife is a good indication of how he will treat the "bride of Christ" or the church. The quality of a man's marriage and family life will reflect his ability to lead the church. This does not mean that a Christian leader must have a perfect home life. But it does mean that he should rule "his own house well" (3:4).

Briefly define the fifteen qualities of a Christian leader outlined by Paul in 1 Timothy 3:1–5 and give your opinion as to why each is important.

1. "blameless"

_____

2. "the husband of one wife"

_____

3. "temperate"

_____

4. "sober-minded"

_____

5. "of good behavior"

_____

6. "hospitable"

_____

7. "able to teach"

_____

8. "not given to wine"

_____

9. "not violent"

_____

10. "not greedy for money"

_____

11. "gentle"

_____

12. "not quarrelsome"

_____

13. "not covetous"

_____

14. "one who rules his own house well"

_____

15. "having his children in all submission with all reverence"

_____

Probing the Depths

The phrase "the husband of one wife" (1 Timothy 3:2) is not referring solely to polygamy. In Ephesus, polygamy was not a real problem and was uncommon in Roman culture. In Roman society, as in our modern-day culture, polygamy was really unnecessary because of easy divorce laws and widespread sexual permissiveness. The actual Greek translation of "the husband of one wife" literally means a "one-woman man." Thus, the Christian leader must be a man who is faithful to his one wife, both mentally and physically.

Read Job 31:1; Matthew 5:27–28; Proverbs 5:1–23.

Question:

What insight have you gained into the importance of faithfulness in marriage?

✎ _____

_____

_____

 Behind the Scenes

The Greek word for bishop, *episkopos*, refers to someone in local pastoral oversight, not the monarchical episcopate of ecclesiastical authority that came later in church history. The word *bishop* translated today would simply mean pastor or elder (Acts 20:28; Titus 1:5–9; 1 Peter 5:1–2). A better word for "bishop" would be "supervisor" or "overseer." *Episkopos* was a Greek term for men who were appointed to regulate the affairs of a city. Two things characterized *episkopos*: (1) oversight over a particular work; (2) accountability to a higher power or authority. This definition gives us insight into the spiritual authority God has given the local pastor. The local pastor has been given charge by God not only for his congregation, but also for the spiritual condition of the community or city in which he lives.

 Kingdom Life—*Conformed to the Image of Christ*

Many believers erroneously assume that the more we grow spiritually, the better we will look to others. The truth is, the more we grow in Christ, the better God looks to others. Paul speaks of the "mystery of godliness" (1 Timothy 3:16) as a series of truths about the Savior. In the same spirit, John the Baptist concisely said, "[Christ] must increase, but I must decrease" (John 3:30).

Practical, personal godliness might be called truth on display, Jesus being the truth. The Father's goal for our lives is to grow us up to be like His Son—to conform us to Christ's image. As our lives tell the truth about God, people who do not know Him will be drawn to faith as they see what He is really like. Godliness is conduct consistent with the character of Christ. Growing in our relationship with God is to become more and more like Christ.

Read Romans 8:29; 1 Corinthians 15:48–49; 2 Corinthians 3:18.

Questions:

In what ways is your ministry "truth on display"?

✎ _____

_____

_____

What areas in your life and ministry remain to be conformed to the image of Christ?

✎ _____

_____

Record Your Thoughts

Questions:

Which of the qualifications for spiritual leadership do you already fulfill?

✎ _____

_____

For which do you want to grow so that you may become better fit to serve as God has called and equipped you?

✎ _____

_____

In what area has the Spirit of God convicted you during your study of this session?

✎ _____

_____

What actions do you intend to take in order to reconcile yourself and your ministry to God?

✎ _____

_____

SESSION TEN

The Good Fight of Faith

1 Timothy 4—6

Kingdom Key—More Than Conquerors

Romans 8:37 Yet in all these things we are more than conquerors through Him who loved us.

Christianity was never meant to be a passive spectator sport. Every Christian must enter life prepared to wage a spiritual battle. The wonderful thing about this battle is that in the end we cannot lose. We may suffer temporary defeats, setbacks, and even failures. But through the blood of Jesus Christ, we can be completely cleansed of failure. We can stand up and fight spiritually even during temporary setbacks. Through relying on the power of the Holy Spirit, we can receive new strength to "fight the good fight of faith" (1 Timothy 6:12). The greater One lives inside us, and He will lead us to victory. In the Christian life and in ministry, we often face struggles where it all seems hopeless. But as we draw upon His strength, we will discover the power to become champions.

Read 1 Samuel 17; Daniel 3; 6:6–28.

Questions:

What attitudes of heart and mind resulted in victory for David, the Hebrew young men, and Daniel?

_____

_____

What might we learn from these accounts of faith?

_____

_____

Probing the Depths

As a spiritual leader, Timothy was to combat the false teaching at Ephesus by teaching sound doctrine and exemplary moral conduct. However, Paul also calls attention to the supernatural aspect of Timothy's ministry, which refers to the time when the elders of Iconium and Lystra laid hands on Timothy and prophesied over him concerning the gifts and callings that God had given him. The New Testament teaches us that there is the laying on of hands with prophecy through which the Holy Spirit can direct and counsel a believer.

Read 1 Corinthians 14:29–32.

Questions:

How can we properly exercise the laying on of hands with prophecy today?

_____

What are some of the guidelines that the Bible gives us regarding prophecy?

_____
_____
_____

What is the role of prophecy in your life and ministry?

_____

Word Wealth—*Eldership*

Eldership: Greek *presbuterion* (pres-boo-ter'-ee-on); Strong's #*4244*: A body of elders (literally aged men), composed of men of dignity, wisdom, and maturity. The word is used of both the Sanhedrin (Luke 22:66 and Acts 22:5) and of Christian presbyters (1 Timothy 4:14).

Kingdom Life—*Guard Your Heart*

The purposes of God need to be thoroughly fastened in our hearts and minds, and we must give our time and attention to them. Matters of importance do not come automatically. Those around us quickly observe the progress we make or the ground we lose.

The personal lives of God's ministers ought to be as pure as their doctrine. The two were made for each other. If the servant of the Lord does not take heed to himself, his doctrine will be sporadic and fuzzy. God's influence can depart from the human heart through carelessness, and our minds can lose the intensity of His call.

Read Philippians 4:4–7; Colossians 3:12–17; 2 John 4–11.

Questions:

What are the tools with which we guard our hearts and minds?

_____

_____

_____

Can you honestly say that you do all "to the glory of God" (1 Corinthians 10:31) in your life and ministry?

_____

_____

_____

What areas need to be surrendered to the Lord in order for your ministry to truly reflect Christ?

_____

_____

_____

True Christianity

True Christianity is not just about prayer, Bible study, worship, and evangelism. The early church was concerned about the practical needs of its people. Our society no longer looks to the church to take care of the poor and needy. We now have a massive state-controlled welfare system. In the early days of Christianity, the church looked after the spiritual and material needs of its people. The apostle Paul also taught believers in Jesus Christ to be as responsible and self-supporting as possible. Paul made it clear that there is a direct relationship between spirituality and the material concerns of life.

There is nothing more tragic than hearing stories about men and women who have served God as ministers of the gospel and who are forced to live in poverty when they retire. The apostle Paul makes it clear that the gospel of Jesus Christ is extremely practical. Those who serve as ministers, Bible teachers, and in other functions of the church should receive a suitable salary for their work. This means that ministers and their families should have such practical things as medical insurance, adequate housing, transportation, and even retirement plans.

Probing the Depths

The truly New Testament–style church promotes leaders wisely and uses appropriate discipline. In our culture today, the church often moves men into positions of leadership prematurely, especially if they have worldly success or fame. Such "celebrity" Christians often fall because they have been elevated into a position for which they are not spiritually ready. In our media-oriented society, this concept of leadership could be extended to any public platform such as singing ministries and television and radio ministries.

Read James 3:1.

Questions:

What is the relationship between character and leadership?

_____

_____

What instances of the danger of faulty character in ministry can you recall in the recent past?

_____

What do you believe led to the fall of these ministers?

✎ _____

_____

_____

What areas of your own character are potentially dangerous to your own ministry? Where might Satan be allowed to find a foothold?

✎ _____

_____

_____

Why do you believe ministers of the gospel will receive a "stricter judgment" (James 3:1)?

✎ _____

_____

_____

Kingdom Life—*Avoid Strife*

Paul clearly taught that sound doctrine should be maintained and defended. He directly confronted the false teachers who were trying to undermine the gospel. However, Paul also warned that some leaders and teachers will fight over minor points of doctrine and simple differences of opinion. They will amplify and exaggerate theological disputes for the sake of furthering their careers, developing a following, and raising money. Paul was warning teachers to steer clear of "arguments over words," "strife," "envy," and "evil suspicions" (1 Timothy 6:4).

Read Proverbs 10:12; 13:10; 15:18; 16:28–30.

Questions:

When others disagree with your theological stance, what is your reaction?

✎ _____

_____

_____

How can you know when you have crossed over the line from defending sound doctrine into simply stirring up strife?

✎ _____

_____

How can you improve in this area?

✎ _____

_____

 Kingdom Life—*Flee Sin; Pursue Godliness*

The Christian leader is not supposed to be caught up in the world's value system of materialism and success. The idea is that the Christian leader is not to seek after money, position, and power in his heart. Instead, he is to pursue "righteousness, godliness, faith, love, patience, gentleness" (1 Timothy 6:11).

The Bible's call to constant maturity is a reminder of God's desire to see us grow up—to mature in His grace and be strengthened to resist temptation. One way we resist temptation is to flee from it. First we flee, then we pursue. Our lives are moving either away from or toward something that summons our interest. When godliness is our goal, we pursue the indisputable values of the born-again lifestyle: righteousness (correct standing before God, demonstrated toward others), faith (thoroughly persuaded of God's truth and totally reliant upon God, manifested toward others), and love (benevolent affection toward God, revealed toward others).

Read Exodus 20:17; James 5:1–6.

Questions:

In what ways has the desire for position or power infected your life and/or ministry?

✎ _____

_____

_____

What things do you truly pursue in your life?

✎ _____

_____

How can wrong pursuits produce personal destruction?

✎ _____

Obstacles

Many people enter some facet of Christian ministry, either part- or full-time, with great enthusiasm and zeal. Then obstacles appear, stressful situations arise, people disappoint them, or rejection sets in, and the enthusiasm suddenly goes out the window. Depression, oppression, and discouragement replace joy. Things can get so bad that ministers feel like quitting their ministries. In addition, very real principalities and powers begin to take advantage of these genuine psychological forces, and all hell can break loose. This is why Paul told us to "fight the good fight of faith" (1 Timothy 6:12).

Read 2 Corinthians 10:3–5; Ephesians 6:10–18.

Questions:

In what ways can we be prepared for obstacles and hindrances in ministry?

✎ _____

What obstacles have you experienced in your life or ministry?

✎ _____

What was your response?

✎ _____

_____

_____

Record Your Thoughts

Spend a few minutes praying and seeking the Lord. Ask the Lord to shine His light into your heart and life. Ask Jesus Christ if there are any areas of covetousness in your life. Then ask the Lord to reveal to you any impure motives in your ministry.

Questions:

Are you in any way seeking money, position, or power instead of His kingdom and His righteousness?

✎ _____

_____

_____

_____

Is there anything in your heart that may be adversely affecting your ministry?

✎ _____

_____

_____

_____

After you have spent a few moments in prayer, confess to the Lord any area in which you feel that your heart is not right or in which you have mixed motives. Ask Him to cleanse you of anything that displeases Him and to change your heart and purify your motives so that loving Him and loving others is top priority.

Finally, as you continue to minister and walk through life, give to the Lord any of these issues if you see them coming up from your heart again. Ask Him to help you become the person of God that He has called you to be.

SESSION ELEVEN

Committed Ministry

2 Timothy

 Kingdom Key—*Know the Word*

Joshua 1:8 This Book of the Law shall not depart from your mouth, but you shall meditate in it day and night, that you may observe to do according to all that is written in it. For then you will make your way prosperous, and then you will have good success.

The Bible—God's inspired Word—is the only conclusive source of wisdom, knowledge, and understanding concerning ultimate realities. It is a fountainhead of freeing truth and a gold mine of practical principles, waiting to liberate and enrich the person who will pursue its truth and wealth. Paul's instruction to be diligent has been applied by serious Christians through the centuries as a directive to study the Word of God. The only way to healthy, balanced living is through "rightly dividing" (2 Timothy 2:15)—Greek *orthotomounta*, literally, "cutting straight"—God's Word. Such correct, straight-on application of God's Word is the result of diligent study. We must go beyond casual approaches to the Scriptures and refuse to suit the Bible to our own convenience or ideology.

The key to staying on course and building churches and ministries as God would have us build them is to be people who intimately know the Word of God and who pray and seek God's face with all our hearts, souls, and minds. If we stay immersed in God's Word and follow hard after Jesus Christ, then whatever outward form the church takes will be guided by Him. After all, it is His church we are building.

Read John 8:32; Psalms 19:10; 119.

Questions:

How much time per day do you devote to reading and studying the Scriptures?

✎ _____

_____

How do you believe this affects the power and stability of your life and ministry?

✎ _____

_____

_____

What things might be hindering your ability to give Scripture its rightful priority in your life?

✎ _____

_____

_____

Kingdom Life—*Discern the Truth*

Paul likens the word of truth to a road being built or a furrow being plowed, both of which must be straight. The good workman must be accurate and clear in his exposition of God's Word, keeping to the road himself and making it easy for others to follow. The "dividing" of the Word of God does not mean to segment it, but to rightly discern its truth by capturing the spirit of the Word.

Read John 6:63; 1 Corinthians 2:13–14; Hebrews 4:12; 2 Peter 2:2.

Questions:

According to other passages you may find, what are the benefits of internalizing the Word of God?

✎ _____

_____

How can knowing the Word of God make it easier for others to follow?

_____

_____

_____

_____

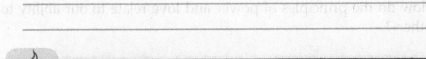

Word Wealth—*Sound Mind*

Sound Mind: Greek *sophronismos* (so-fron-is-moss'); Strong's #*4995*: A combination of *sos*, "safe," and *phren*, "the mind"; hence, safe-thinking. The word denotes good judgment, disciplined thought patterns, the ability to understand and make right decisions, and self-discipline. Literally this word means saving the mind through admonishing and calling to soundness of mind and to self-control. One of the attributes that an effective Christian leader must have is the ability to make the right decisions. A sound mind is essential in making this process work.

Kingdom Life—*Do Not Waver*

Second Timothy has been called a handbook for young ministers of the gospel. Paul wrote this letter to Timothy to give him instructions regarding the welfare of the church, its organization, and ways to safeguard the gospel. This letter was not written from some theological ivory tower. Paul wrote in chains from the confines of a dungeon inside a Roman prison. With very little provision, Paul not only witnessed to his fellow inmates, but he also continued in his ministry. As a spiritual father to Timothy, Paul needed to confront something in Timothy's personality that could inhibit his full potential in ministry—Timothy's tendency to waver. This is why Paul exhorted Timothy with the words, "God has not given us a spirit of fear, but of power and of love and of a sound mind" (2 Timothy 1:7).

Timothy, like many people in ministry today, was prone to fear and may have been reluctant to accept heavy responsibilities. As a true father in the faith, Paul dealt with these issues in Timothy's life and encouraged Timothy to exercise the principle of a sound mind.

Read Proverbs 3:1–26; James 1:5–8.

Questions:

How does fear inhibit our ability to make the right decisions?

_____

_____

How do the principles of power and love relate to our ability to lead others?

_____

_____

Why is having a sound mind essential to effective ministry?

_____

How can you develop a sound mind?

_____

Kingdom Life—Do Not Water Down the Gospel

In our relativistic culture, there is constant pressure to dilute the power of the gospel. In addition there is the ever-present temptation to dress up the gospel or to wrap it in contemporary terms to make it more palatable to the society around us. But the apostle Paul warns us against making such a mistake. The truth is what sets people free. To dilute the Word of God is to deny its power and will result in lost ministries and lost lives. Although this message is foolishness to the world, only the full, powerful Word of God can save and transform people's lives.

Read 1 Corinthians 1:18–25; Romans 1:16–17.

Questions:

What lies at the heart of the temptation to dilute the gospel?

_____

_____

_____

As a minister in the kingdom, what should be your response when people suggest that you tone down your message or make it more acceptable to a wider audience?

✎ _____

_____

_____

Have you ever succumbed to any fear of proclaiming the truth?

✎ _____

_____

_____

What is your view of that act in view of this study?

✎ _____

_____

_____

Models for Strong Ministry

Metaphors are a great teaching tool. They require that we truly ponder their meaning and give us a mental picture with which to equate the truth contained. In writing about developing a strong ministry, Paul uses the metaphors of a soldier, an athlete, and a farmer.

Read 2 Timothy 2:1–6.

Questions:

How can applying the principles of the following metaphors strengthen your ministry?

✎ _____

_____

"Be strong in the grace that is in Christ Jesus" (2 Timothy 2:1).

✎ _____

"Endure hardship as a good soldier of Jesus Christ" (2:3).

_____

_____

_____

"No one engaged in warfare entangles himself with the affairs of this life" (2:4).

_____

_____

_____

"If anyone competes in athletics, he is not crowned unless he competes according to the rules" (2:5).

_____

_____

_____

"The hardworking farmer must be first to partake in the crops" (2:6).

_____

_____

_____

Probing the Depths

In the late nineteenth century, the acceptance of higher critical methods of studying Scripture developed first by a number of German theologians began to gain popularity among some Christian denominations here in the United States. "Criticism" of the Bible means analysis and interpretation. Lower, or textual, criticism seeks to establish the most accurate Greek and Hebrew texts of the Bible. Higher criticism arises from lower criticism (these terms are not used widely today), and it concerns itself with questions regarding who, when, where, and how.

Depending on the faith commitment of the Bible scholar, either the various higher-critical approaches can root our faith more deeply in a historically accurate understanding of the world and words of the Bible, or they can be used to dismantle historic biblical faith. Faith is no friend of ignorance, and the proper use of many critical approaches has produced the study guides, Bible dictionaries, and commentaries that all Bible students rely on to help them rightly divide the Word of Truth.

Unfortunately, however, much use of higher criticism has not so much enlightened as it has undercut the authority, divine inspiration, and inerrancy of the Scriptures. In the hands of scholars who do not submit their personal beliefs to the authority of God's written Word, these critical methods end up placing merely human opinions, ideas, and philosophies on par with or above biblical truth. When this happens, biblical truth is treated as only one classic opinion or tradition among many. This approach to truth results in moral relativism and nonbiblical ideas about God and man. Consequently, certain quarters of the church have been robbed of their power to stand for holiness and biblical truth in the midst of a culture that is in a moral free fall. What we teach and believe matters in the real world because it has profound consequences in the lives of people. And wherever people resist God and His truth written in Scripture, they choose error for their guide.

Vessels in God's Service

Paul states, "But in a great house there are not only vessels of gold and silver, but also of wood and clay, some for honor and some for dishonor" (2 Timothy 2:20). The term "great house" refers to the church of God, the body of Christ. The idea is that believers and Christian leaders can determine if they will be honorable or dishonorable vessels in God's service. According to Paul, the key to being a "vessel for honor" (2:21) is to allow ourselves to be cleansed by the sanctifying power of the Holy Spirit. We become sanctified by the power of the Spirit as we pursue and seek Jesus.

Read John 17:17–19; Acts 26:18; 1 Corinthians 1:2; Hebrews 10:10.

Questions:

What does it mean to be sanctified?

✎ _____

_____

_____

What specific ways can you obey Paul's exhortation to pursue righteousness?

_____

_____

Faith?

_____

Love?

_____

Peace?

_____

_____

After studying the following definition of *sanctified*, write a short description in your own words of how this work of the Holy Spirit can be produced in your own life.

_____

_____

Word Wealth—*Sanctified*

Sanctified: Greek *hagiazo* (hag-ee-ad'-zo); Strong's #37: *Hagiazo* means "to hallow, set apart, dedicate, consecrate, separate, sanctify, make holy." *Hagiazo*, as a state of holiness, is opposite of *koinon*, common or unclean. In the Old Testament, things, places, and ceremonies were named *hagiazo*. In the New Testament, the word describes a manifestation of life produced by the indwelling Holy Spirit. Because the Father set Him apart, Jesus is appropriately called the Holy One of God (Mark 1:24).

Kingdom Life—*Finish the Race*

About thirty years after his supernatural encounter with Jesus Christ on the Damascus road, Paul was finishing the course that the Lord had set before him. Knowing full well that his life would be over soon, Paul gave some final instructions to Timothy and the church. Paul had offered up his life to God and was "being poured out as a drink offering" (2 Timothy 4:6; see Numbers 15:1–10). But Paul did not fear death. He said confidently, "There is laid up for me the crown of righteousness" (2 Timothy 4:8). "Crown" translates the Greek word *stephanos*. A *stephanos* was the wreath given to winning athletes. Paul fully expected to be rewarded by God because he had been obedient to the call.

Read Philippians 3:12–14.

Questions:

What qualities or activities are necessary to be diligent in your pursuit of the kingdom?

_____

_____

_____

_____

What prizes might we experience in the here and now as a result of pursuing the kingdom?

_____

_____

_____

_____

Record Your Thoughts

In 2 Timothy Paul gave us the groundwork for motivation in ministry. A minister of the gospel is a servant of God's Word—both the prophetic,contemporary Word, and the recorded, written Word. From reading Paul's closing comments (2 Timothy 4:9–22), we elicit a message about what is required of all who are called into ministry and the Christian life itself. That message is that we are to fight the good fight, finish the race, and keep the faith.

Questions:

In your own words write how you can become the servant that God wants you to be.

_____

_____

_____

_____

How do you now see your motivation for ministry?

_____

_____

_____

_____

What do you need to do to become a more effective and faithful soldier?

_____

_____

_____

_____

What would you like God to do for you?

_____

_____

_____

SESSION TWELVE

Renewal

Titus

 Kingdom Key—*A Champion of Grace*

Ephesians 2:8–9 By grace you have been saved through faith, and that not of yourselves; it is the gift of God, not of works, lest anyone should boast.

Titus calls us to be champions of grace, diligently teaching that good works cannot save us. Yet we are equally to be champions of godly living, giving clear guidelines for righteous conduct and behavior. Grace is never to be an excuse for ungodly living, but we are to live in godliness because Jesus has forgiven us and set us free by His grace. God's grace and the power of His Spirit enable us to lead peaceful, godly lives in humility and truth.

Read Proverbs 3:34; John 1:14–17; Acts 4:33; 20:32; Romans 5:12–21.

Questions:

How do you define *grace*?

_____

_____

Of all the virtues of Christ, why is grace of prime importance to the believer?

_____

_____

How can grace be an active part of your life and ministry?

_____

_____

Legalism

Those who desire to walk and minister in the strength and Spirit of Jesus must understand that legalism actually disqualifies one from good works. To act out of perceived obligation is contrary to the law of love as taught by our Savior. Good works are born of grace; they are to be the response of our hearts and minds to the grace of Jesus. When we do things out of legalism to try to earn salvation or favor with God, essentially we are saying that Christ's work on the cross was not enough.

Behind the Scenes

Paul wrote his epistle to Titus around A.D. 64. Although there is no mention of Titus in the Acts of the Apostles, Titus was a close companion and valuable coworker of Paul. As a young preacher of the gospel, Titus traveled with Paul extensively and accompanied Paul and Barnabas to the Council of Jerusalem. Paul gave Titus the assignment of directing the young churches on the island of Crete. This letter to Titus gave him practical instructions concerning the performance of pastoral duties and the handling of difficulties and problems related to leadership.

The island of Crete was 160 miles long, situated strategically near Greece and Asia Minor. Titus had his work cut out for him. He had to deal with the "insubordinate, both idle talkers and deceivers" (Titus 1:10). In addition, the Cretans had a reputation for being "liars, evil beasts, lazy gluttons" (1:12). The expression "you Cretan" is still used today as a derogatory term.

Kingdom Life—*Learn to Lead*

The primary role of the Christian leader is teaching. He is to instruct others in godly living, regardless of his station in life. Also, he is to guard God's church from false teachers and deceivers who take advantage of the people of God. The godly leader's teaching is to be first through the life that he lives: People should be able to look at the Christian leader and say, "That is how I am supposed to live." Also he needs to be an able communicator of truth.

A true leader in the body of Christ should:

1. *Not lead alone.* Rather, he or she is to involve other faithful, qualified persons to help them minister to the people of God.
2. *Silence the rebellious.* In order to protect the body of Christ, a godly leader must identify and sharply rebuke those whose lives are only talk and who seek to deceive others.
3. *Teach and encourage others.* Take an active role in teaching others how to live self-controlled, exemplary, and fruitful lives.
4. *Teach by example.* Exemplify excellent character and self-control. Do not allow your actions to provide an occasion for accusation.

Read 1 Corinthians 13.

Questions:

How does each of the attributes of love manifest in a true godly ministry?

✎_____

_____

How might these attributes be employed to bring relational and spiritual health to a local body?

✎_____

_____

In which of these areas do you find your life and/or ministry lacking?

✎_____

_____

What steps can you take to remedy this?

✎_____

_____

Saturday Evening of Time

If all time were represented as a seven-day week, most would agree that we are living in the Saturday evening of time. Signs abound all around us that time is short and the return of our Lord is imminent.

The greatest sign of all is that the gospel of the kingdom will be preached throughout all the earth, and this is precisely what is happening in our day in an unprecedented manner. In fact, 70 percent of all world evangelism has taken place since the year 1900, and 70 percent of that progress has happened since World War II. It is interesting to note that the greatest explosion of world evangelism has happened since Israel became a nation again in 1948. All across the globe, millions are accepting Jesus Christ as their Lord and Savior as never before. Since the fall of Communism in Russia, multiple millions have come to Christ. The same is true in Communist China.

There are many different views of the timing and coming events surrounding the end of time and the return of our Lord. Believers in Jesus should never break fellowship about such things. Mature Christians can have different viewpoints as to the timing of such events as the Rapture, the Tribulation, and the Second Coming. Teaching sound doctrine requires that we teach such biblical themes as the Second Coming, the Millennium, the Great Tribulation, and other aspects of eschatology (the study of last things).

Questions:

What does it mean that we should "live soberly" (Titus 2:12)?

What are the dangers of conjecture and date setting regarding eschatology?

How is discipleship and godly living a vital part of teaching on the "blessed hope" (2:13)?

In what ways should the recognition of our Lord's imminent return affect your life and ministry?

✎ _____

_____

_____

_____

Word Wealth—*Soberly*

Soberly: Greek *sophronos* (so-fron'-oce); Strong's #4996: Derived from *sozo,* "to save," and *phren,* "the mind." This word is an adverb signifying acting in a responsible manner, sensibly, prudently, being in self-control and in full possession of intellectual and emotional faculties.

The apostle Paul exhorts believers to live "soberly" (Titus 2:12). He is not talking about a dour-faced, legalistic, and joyless form of Christianity. He is telling us to live sensibly in an insensible age. This sobriety should be reflected in our teaching on such matters as eschatology and the Holy Spirit. Again, this does not mean that we cannot become excited or enthusiastic. Nor does it mean that we cannot be open to the Holy Spirit's moving in fullness and power. We can experience the fullness and renewing power of the Holy Spirit while at the same time being in full possession of intellectual and emotional faculties.

Kingdom Life—*Build a Sound Church*

Listed below are key characteristics of a sound church. Study the descriptions and think of ways each would strengthen and build a sound church. Circle the four behaviors you would like your local church to cultivate. Present these to God in prayer and ask Him how they might be accomplished. In cooperation with the leadership of your church, be ready to do what the Holy Spirit lays on your heart. Then put a check mark next to the behavior you most need to cultivate in your spiritual life. Submit yourself to the Word and to the opportunities God will bring for you to grow in this area.

Characteristics of a Sound Church (Titus 2:1–10)

Sober	Sound in faith	Reverent
Sound in love	Not slanderers	Temperate
Not given to much wine	Teachers	Discreet
Obedient	Chaste	Sober-minded
Good works	Integrity	Sound speech

 ## Kingdom Life—*Willingly Accept the Spirit's Leading*

Second Corinthians, 1 and 2 Timothy, and Titus all teach the importance of sound doctrine. But sound doctrine alone does not produce spiritual fruitfulness and revival, nor does simply having the right doctrine build a church. There are many churches that seem to preach sound doctrine but have little life in them. This does not minimize the absolute importance of having sound doctrine. But a living church must also have the fresh move of the Holy Spirit in order to be all that Jesus intends it to be. In Titus 3:5 Paul used the phrase "renewing of the Holy Spirit." He urged all believers to be constantly open to the fresh outpourings of the Holy Spirit "whom He poured out on us abundantly" (3:6). This involves a decision of our will. We must be truly willing to experience a fresh move of God's Spirit and revival.

Read Romans 8:14; Proverbs 11:14; 24:6.

Questions:

Are you continually sensitive to the promptings of the Holy Spirit in your life and ministry?

_____

How does this affect your walk and ministry?

_____

Do you often seek confirmation from others as you follow the leading of the Holy Spirit?

_____

_____

_____

What might be gained from this practice?

_____

_____

_____

Kingdom Extra

We can participate in the Holy Spirit's renewal of our lives as individuals and churches. *Renewing* comes from the word *anakainosis,* which is a combination of *ana* "again," and *kainos* "new." The word suggests a renovation, restoration, transformation, and a change of heart and life. In Romans 12:2, it indicates a complete change for the better, an adjustment of one's moral and spiritual vision. Here it stresses the work of the Holy Spirit in transforming the life of every believer.

Read Romans 12:2.

Questions:

In what ways can the following terms positively affect your ministry?

New

_____

_____

_____

Renovation

_____

Restoration

✎ _____

_____

_____

_____

Transformation

✎ _____

_____

_____

_____

Record Your Thoughts

God is sending His glory and revival all over our world today.

Questions:

How can we be sure that we are open to the revival God wants to bring about in our hearts without succumbing to pride or a loss of sound doctrine?

✎ _____

_____

_____

How can we maintain openness for revival and renewal without surrendering to fanaticism or pure emotionalism?

✎ _____

_____

_____

As our world is being flooded with the glory of God, there seem to be many different streams of God's blessing and revival. How can we avoid the subtle pride that can occur by being preoccupied with what God is doing in our own church or movement to the exclusion of the body of Christ at large?

✎ _____

_____

_____

_____

As revival comes, how can we protect a truly interdenominational spirit and avoid a small-minded sectarianism?

✎ _____

_____

_____

_____

When we see an outbreak of unusual signs and manifestations, how can we avoid the trap of being excessively critical without losing our discernment?

✎ _____

_____

_____

_____

How can we stay open to the miraculous without being overly preoccupied with signs?

✎ _____

_____

_____

_____

How can we stay on the road of the spiritual cutting edge without falling into the ditches of superspirituality and sloppy doctrine or of doctrinal soundness that is as straight as a gun barrel and just as empty?

✎ _____

_____

_____

Conclusion

We have been made holy to live holy lives. God's grace teaches us to do good works not to earn salvation, but because we are free from sinful behavior and free to do good things for God. This is the privilege and inheritance of God's people, not a harsh law to be followed and fulfilled. Holy living is the response of God's chosen and special people to the redeeming love and immeasurable grace of Jesus.

We must understand that Jesus rescued us from evil and from repeatedly falling into sin. He made us holy. He made us to burn with zeal and enthusiasm to do good works by His grace.

Probing the Depths—*Review*

Review your life and ministry in light of the twelve Kingdom Keys of this lesson. Consider how each is manifested in your service to the Lord and how you might grow in effectiveness as you allow the Spirit of God to mature you in each of these areas.

1. Weakness = Strength

_____

_____

_____

2. Triumph in Christ

_____

_____

_____

3. Be God's Tool

_____

_____

4. It's All About Jesus

_____

_____

_____

5. **Glorify God**

_____

_____

_____

6. **Walk in Humility**

_____

_____

7. **Decrease into Greatness**

_____

_____

_____

8. **Be Enabled**

_____

_____

_____

9. **Be Diligent**

_____

_____

10. **More Than Conquerors**

_____

_____

_____

11. **Know the Word**

_____

_____

_____

12. A Champion of Grace

✎ _____

_____

_____

May our Lord greatly empower you to minister in the strength and Spirit of Jesus.

Be zealous and do good things for God!

Printed in the USA
CPSIA information can be obtained
at www.ICGtesting.com
JSHW031926200424
61596JS00005B/32